Pop Life

Pop Life

A Journey By Sofa

Caspar Llewellyn Smith

S

SCEPTRE

The author has quoted from 'Evergreen' (Westlife, copyright 2003 Irish Records) and 'I Wanna Be Adored' (The Stone Roses, copyright 1989 Silvertone)

Copyright © 2002 by Caspar Llewellyn Smith

First published in Great Britain in 2002 by Hodder and Stoughton
A division of Hodder Headline

The right of Caspar Llewellyn Smith to be identified as the Author of the Work has been asserted by him in accordance with the Copyright, Designs and Patents Act 1988.

A Sceptre paperback

1 3 5 7 9 10 8 6 4 2

All rights reserved. No part of this publication may be reproduced, stored in a retrieval system, or transmitted, in any form or by any means without the prior written permission of the publisher, nor be otherwise circulated in any form of binding or cover other than that in which it is published and without a similar condition being imposed on the subsequent purchaser.

A CIP catalogue record for this title is available
from the British Library

ISBN 0 340 82633 9

Typeset in Sabon by Palimpsest Book Production Limited,
Polmont, Stirlingshire

Printed and bound in Great Britain by
Clays Ltd, St Ives plc

Hodder and Stoughton
A division of Hodder Headline
338 Euston Road
London NW1 3BH

For Zoë, Sam and Esme
together forever

Contents

1. The Week the World Went Pop (and I Went with It) — 1
2. Pop in Crisis and the Problem with Hear'Say — 22
3. My Pop Life — 40
4. *Big Brother* and How TV Went Pop — 88
5. Celebrity Culture and *Heat* — 110
6. The Birth of Our Pop Phenomenon — 128
7. The Birth of Pop Culture — 145
8. *Pop Idol* — 174
9. The Secret of Success — 195
10. Pete Waterman is God aka Words I Thought I Would Never Write — 216
11. The Real Reason I Loved *Pop Idol* — 229

Epilogue: And in the End — 253

Author's Note: Records To Listen To While Writing a Book — 256

Bibliography — 259

Pop Life

1

THE WEEK THE WORLD WENT POP
(AND I WENT WITH IT)

> *'I have used so many wonderful expletives about you but I saw one better tonight – Will, I'm British and I love you'* – Pete Waterman

In the first ten days of February 2002, Britain was gripped by *Pop Idol*. The Thames Television/19TV talent show dominated the tabloid news agenda and filled the glossy pages of magazines like *Heat* and *Now*. The audience of BBC's *Question Time* wanted to know which contender the panel supported. Broadsheet commentators wondered what our experience of Gareth, Will and Darius could teach a modern democracy. A man called Malcolm Evans, director of 'semiotic insight' at a marketing agency specialising in something called brand repositioning, asked, 'Why not let voters choose their own favourite political idol each week?'

Here's a measure of just how silly things became: in the week of the *Pop Idol* final, the biggest bona fide pop star on the planet, Britney Spears, pretended to be a contestant from the series for the sake of a skit on Frank Skinner's TV chat show. In the week of the *Pop Idol* final, one of the judges, Pete Waterman, dined privately with the Prime Minister. 'I wish we could get the middle classes to vote for us like they do for *Pop Idol*,' said Tony to Pete, apparently.

Each week millions of people had rung the show to vote for their favourite contestant. Bookies recorded a flood of bets on who would finally win, with William Hill reporting far greater interest in the show than in something like *Big Brother*. It seemed that no one in the land was safe from *Pop Idol* fever. Not even me.

To my surprise – and horror – I too was sucked into all this madness. I thought I couldn't care less. I couldn't have been more wrong.

It was an average week for real news, focusing on the government's battle to convince parents that the MMR vaccine is safe. I was one of the parents worried about it. But I was almost more concerned that Sam (three) and Esme (one) might grow up in a world where Gareth Gates had won.

On Friday 1st, the *Sun* led its front page with an exclusive phone poll which showed Darius coming second. This meant 'the unbelievable could happen – the *Popstars* reject WINNING the contest'. Darius Danesh had been the subject of national ridicule when he had been booted off *Popstars*, the show in whose image *Pop Idol* was most obviously founded, following a ball-mangling performance of Britney's 'Baby One More Time'. It had taken courage to apply to the new show and then, somehow, he'd made it past the mass auditions for ten thousand wannabes, through two further rounds, past seven other finalists and into the last three.

I say somehow because my girlfriend, Zoë, had got it right when she said he was and always had been and would remain a real creep. The messianic egotist had lost the absurd facial hair that had made him look like a member of the happy-clappy brigade; but the fuzz, it turned out, had actually been helping. Without it, that beatific grin looked all the more like the product of years spent in the company of evangelical snake-oil salesmen. Nonetheless, here he was with 27.5 per cent of the *Sun*'s readers' votes. Will Young languished on 17.5 per cent. Gareth Gates bestrode the contest with a commanding 55 per cent. G-g-go, Gareth . . .

There were two other stories of interest to me in that same issue of the paper. One concerned another TV programme: 'Star Gary Lucy is dating a Page 3 girl – just like his character in the hit telly show *Footballers' Wives*.' I had never seen *Footballers' Wives*, I just liked this intermingling of real life with fantasy. The other was a full-page essay by the television editor asking why TV bosses were scared of new ideas. The writer scolded the BBC and ITV for feeding viewers with a diet of has-beens and rehashes. 'The only real innovation is reality TV,' she added. '*Big Brother*, *Soapstars*, *Popstars*, *Pop Idol*, *Temptation Island* – the list goes on ad nauseam.' There was that same blurring.

On Saturday 2nd, Darius was knocked out. We were ecstatic. But the *coup de grâce* came when our cheeky-chappie presenters, Ant and Dec, revealed just before the credits rolled that there was only half a per cent between the remaining two in their race for this title. Suddenly, from nowhere . . . come on, Will!

I don't think Will would ever qualify for my idea of a pop idol. The Berkshire-born twenty-three-year-old seemed too polite and middle class. His dad was a company director and at eight he had been sent to Horris Hill boarding school ('a good all-rounder and head chorister', according to the headmaster). Then Wellington, though having cocked up his A-levels he went to a sixth-form college in Oxford for retakes. Two As and a B in Politics, Ancient History and English later, he headed west, to Exeter University, where he took a 2:2 in politics. And nothing there seemed very cool.

Will had starred in a student production of *Oklahoma!* – photos of which were now trundled out in celebrity magazines – and after leaving university he enrolled in the Arts Educational School in Chiswick, west London. Well, I'd watched *Fame* too, as a kid, but I didn't fancy a life wearing leggings, learning how to sing and dance. And it didn't seem to me that real pop idols went about their business that way either.

The Young family was clearly wealthy, but Will had gone £11,000 in debt to get through university and the first year at drama school looked like costing him a further £10,000. I guess there was something to admire in that determination. But aren't pop idols born the way they are? It's not supposed to be a skill that you pay to learn.

Then *Pop Idol* came calling. Or rather, Will saw the

application form in the *News of the World* in June 2001, and filled it in.

The seventeen-year-old Gareth seemed more like the real deal, though that was partly because he looked as if you could peer through one ear and right out again through the other, like with most modern pop performers. But in fairness he was a bright lad, the son of a postman from Bradford with seven As and three Bs at GCSE and a place on offer at the Royal Northern College of Music in Manchester. On closer inspection it turned out that he had once been the head choirboy at Bradford Cathedral. That didn't seem too promising either, then. But I could see a Saturday night TV audience voting for him. It helped, of course, that Gareth stammered – and sang just like an angel.

The final week of *Pop Idol* was pitched as a political campaign between the two. Both candidates drew up a list of pledges – such as 'I pledge not to become a music industry diva and not to request lychees on tap 24/7' (Will) or 'I pledge to work hard and give my fans everything they deserve' (Gareth).

Monday. At 5.30 a.m., two battle buses equipped with their own bunk beds and 'chill-out areas' picked the boys up. Each contestant travelled with his own entourage, including a personal assistant, a press officer, a *Pop Idol* producer, an official photographer, members of the TV crew and a hair and make-up lady. Will went to GMTV to give an interview, while Gareth headed straight to the *Big Breakfast*. Then it was off to Wapping to see the *Sun* and the *News of the World* before busing over to the *Express* building, followed by an afternoon of TV interviews. Will did thirteen in the course of four hours. Then both candidates went off to Capital Radio to meet 'Dr' Neil Fox, who was also a *Pop Idol* judge, for a final interview live on air.

Tuesday. Both boys had a lie-in until half eight before battle again began. Will went to *This Morning* for another TV appearance, then carried out some broadsheet interviews, before going over to Radio 2 for a chat with Steve Wright. In the afternoon, both did more press, which included an encounter with Michael White, the political editor of the *Guardian*. White told Gareth to take encouragement in what seemed like a hindered bid for stardom from the fact that Nye Bevan had a stammer and Churchill suffered from a lisp. 'He appears to have heard of neither of these recording artists,' he reported, however. 'And why should he, I suppose. They are both very dead.'

After that, it was off to Broadcasting House for an interview on Radio 1 with Chris Moyles, then more interviews, with the *Observer*, *The Times*, the *Independent* and the *Sunday Mirror*.

I had quietly spent that morning wandering round the Andy Warhol retrospective at Tate Modern, with *Pop Idol* on my mind. The obvious speculation involved Gareth and Will and their fifteen minutes of fame. Instead I was struck by Gareth's likeness to Elvis in one of Warhol's double silk-screened portraits. It wasn't simply the hint of a snarl and the same jet-black hair they shared . . . there was also some otherworldly presence there.

I must have lost the plot.

How could anyone think like that about Gareth?

Because despite my doubts – for reasons I'm not sure I fully understood – I'd long-since decided Will was the one for me. I couldn't waver now.

Wednesday. The boys were up at five and did three hours of phone interviews with local radio stations across the nation, then more press. In the afternoon, they went to the recording of Graham Norton's TV chat show to film him tossing a coin to see who would perform first on Saturday's final.

'They were an exhausting three days,' said Julian Henry from the PR company Henry's House, who organised everything. 'But,' he added, 'the boys were all right.' On the Thursday, Will and Gareth went into rehearsals, readying themselves for the big day. The *Sun* decided to stir things up, asking *Pop Idol* bosses to answer ten 'vital' questions about the show. There was a general perception that the series had been somehow weighted in Gareth's favour, so the paper's showbiz editor wanted to know:

1. Why was the first single chosen weeks ago when the remaining candidates had such different voices?
2. Why was Gareth allowed to sing Westlife's 'Flying Without Wings' on Saturday night's

show when we had already heard him sing it earlier in the series?
3. Why is the first single a cover of an old song instead of being a new track?
4. Why does Gareth only seem to stutter when he is live on the show?
5. How can the show be fair when Simon Cowell, Simon Fuller and Nicky [sic] Chapman have such vested interests?

And so on, culminating in 'Is it all a fix designed to leave Gareth the winner?'. The single 'chosen weeks ago' was a cover of a track by Irish pop poltroons Westlife, 'Evergreen', which Gareth, Will and Darius had recorded ten days earlier, together with 'Anything Is Possible', a new song written by former pop star Cathy Dennis. The idea was that whoever won the series would have a double A-side ready for release within a fortnight.

Simon Fuller was the head of 19, a company that managed S Club 7 and other million-selling pop acts. He had dreamt up *Pop Idol* with Simon Cowell, an A&R man at BMG, the record division of the German media group Bertelsmann. Cowell worked with acts like Westlife and was also a *Pop Idol* judge. Nicki Chapman had known Cowell for years, and worked for Fuller. She was the third judge. It did all start to look suspect... The *Pop Idol* prize was a management deal with Fuller and Chapman and a record contract with Cowell.

On Friday, the *Sun* revealed that both finalists – Gareth and Will – would take the prize, whatever the outcome of Saturday's show. It looked like a scandal of staggering magnitude . . .

The paper also found room to report that Wendy Gates had rung the showbiz editor to say she was upset at 'viewers' suggestions' that Gareth, her son, was faking his speech impediment.

That evening, we stayed up past our bedtime to see the Graham Norton show. Will won the coin-toss. The omens looked good.

Saturday dawned mild. Sir Cliff Richard, 'God' and the British Stammering Association were reported to be backing Gareth. Posh (Victoria Beckham) and Robbie (Williams) were reported to have voted for our boy. 'Will it be Will?' asked the *Sun*, reporting a groundswell in favour of our young man.

Yet the picture that dominated the front page was of Gareth. And I still couldn't in my heart of hearts believe that it wouldn't be him who triumphed.

The tension was building. An editorial in the *Daily Telegraph* declared: 'The votes that the nation is today being asked to cast will affect the future not only of the candidates but of us all . . . Is it right at a time like this that the Prime Minister should be swanning off to Africa as if the fate of Gareth and Will were of little importance?'

This kind of coverage was exactly what Simon Fuller and Julian Henry had been hoping for. In previous weeks they had achieved what they termed critical mass with the tabloids – hence stories like the one about Eileen and Cedric Salter of Colwyn Bay, North Wales, who named ten newborn puppies after *Pop Idol*'s final ten contestants. But now the serious papers were on board too.

For the best *Pop Idol* coverage I could only turn to *Heat*, however. When *Pop Idol* was being planned, Simon Cowell told Simon Fuller that if the magazine got behind the show it would be a success. That week, they gave *Pop Idol* eleven pages of coverage, leading with speculation that Gareth and Zoe Birkett, the last contestant kicked off the show before Darius, were dating. They also broke news that Will's family had been acting like bounders, quoting Wendy Gates again as saying, 'I've noticed in the last few weeks that they never clap after Gareth's performances.'

Well, I'm middle class. To me that seemed a rather normal middle-class reaction – born of embarrassment at being filmed live in the studio, not malice. All the same, William's mother, Annabel, angrily denied the accusation. Will had bumped into the editor of the magazine on Friday, as it happened, and had had stern words, apparently.

My sister and her boyfriend came round for the final. We decided to video the show so we could put the children to bed in peace and watch the programme later. It was our usual routine, if fraught with danger. One Saturday night, we had made a rare sortie off the sofa and out of the house to dinner. Coming back later, we sent the babysitter home and rewound the tape to the start of the programme. And watched the thing. Calamity! By the time it had finished, we were too late to see the short show later that same evening revealing which contestant had scored the fewest votes and had been eliminated from the contest. I spent half an hour on Teletext and Ceefax trying to find out the result.

We timed it all perfectly this time, so the main programme finished just before the start of the live update at 10.05 p.m. Later, we learnt that the main show had trashed its rivals in the ratings that night – a Hollywood film on BBC1 and *Top 10: Duets* on Channel 4 – pulling in an astonishing 13.9 million viewers.

For the climax of the eighteen-week series, the judges dropped all the snide remarks and nasty comments that had previously been their trademark, and wore black tie. They lavished Gareth and Will with praise. Pete Waterman memorably told the latter: 'I have used so many wonderful expletives about you but I saw one better tonight – Will, I'm British and I love you.'

The boys could each pick a song that they had sung earlier in the series. Gareth chose the old faithful 'Unchained Melody', and raised goose pimples, quite frankly. I'm quite a vocal TV watcher, and had been shouting a lot about how rubbish Gareth was and how he looked a durr-brain. But now the time to criticise was over. Brilliant.

Will picked 'Light My Fire' by The Doors. Incendiary! Better. For one thing, Will had live flames shooting across the studio when he reached the final chorus . . . Both sang 'Anything Is Possible' and 'Evergreen'. We'd grown used to hearing classics throughout the course of *Pop Idol* and it was difficult to pay attention to two new songs. New to me anyway – I'd never heard the Westlife one before. But between Will and Gareth's performances on the night, it seemed to us that there could only be one winner. Bring it on!

I was full of hope now. What's more, like millions of others, we had calculated that Will would pick up the bulk of Darius's votes from the previous week, because Darius fans were more likely Will than Gareth fans (alarmingly). I imagined that teenage girls had been voting for Gareth all along and that he'd been coming out top in the votes each week quite comfortably. But as the series went on, older viewers, with more mature tastes, were likely to have started watching too. (I'd been vociferous enough in recommending it to people.) Could we dare let hope blossom?

In the two hours between the first and second programmes, the national grid had called ITV to check advertising break times, fearing power cuts if there was a huge surge in electricity demand when people went to put the kettle on. British Telecom – BT, whatever – reported that their 28,000 phone lines for the votes were besieged with up to one million callers every second. Phone overload caused chaos for the Beds and Herts Ambulance Service, where controllers were unable to reach any ambulance stations in outlying towns in the counties during that period.

To be honest, I had never participated in something like this before, staying my hand by the phone through

Big Brother, *Big Brother 2* and *Celebrity Big Brother*, though I had avidly watched them all. I had never voted before in *Pop Idol*. Now I rang, four times: Will; Will; Will; Will. My sister used her mobile to let the others join in. (Where would programmes like *Pop Idol* and *Big Brother* be without the new mobile phone culture?)

Showtime. Will and Gareth stood side by side. The final result was in. In the end 8.7 million calls had been received, obliterating the British record for a TV phone-in vote. And one contestant had bagged 4.6 million, giving him a 53.1 per cent share, which of course made him the winner. And that winner was . . .

Will.

Will!!!!

Even as we screamed – not a pretty sight, with gobbets of spittle flying from me – Will had walked away from Ant and Dec, picked up a mic and launched straight into 'Evergreen' again. Cool. And in truth – hand on heart – first time round it had sounded like a piece of plastic cheese. But now the lyrics took on a new resonance. 'I'm going to take this night,' he crooned, 'And make it evergreen.' Ahhh . . . we thought, belatedly recognising the shrewdness of the sentiments, and the cynicism involved in the selection of the song, and not really minding.

But there wasn't time to think, because as Will was singing every other kid from the series' final fifty had trooped on from the wings to sing backing vocals. It was meant to be a bit like the finale to Live Aid, I guess. In fact it seemed a touch karaoke.

When the song ended, however, everyone tried to mob the nation's pop idol in a spontaneous gesture of goodwill, and it was pretty touching. Darius didn't try to throttle him, as I had feared.

For us at home, it was a particular pleasure to see Will there, suddenly hoisted on the shoulders of the others, because it was us who had really put him there, through voting. And then came a moment I shan't ever forget.

The camera closes in on Will and Gareth. They look as if they've sucked up all the energy in the whole pop universe. The only two to make it to the final show – it seems as if a truth denied the others passes between them as their eyes lock. Then Will's head slumps forward.

He looks utterly lost in the moment, thinking back to everything that has gone before in his life, and forward to the realisation that seems to dawn for the first time that, from this instant, everything will change for him for ever. We went to bed, and I wondered whether the world would be different for us too. There was a lot to dream on there.

> 'You ought to see my TV, it's covered in spit' – Liam Gallagher

Pop Idol was a modern phenomenon and a strange turn of events in more ways than one. I had watched

Popstars like a teen pop fan. I had watched every series of *Big Brother* with the fanaticism of an Afghan mujahid. The new programme looked like a hybrid of the two. It also seemed to spring from the same culture. *Big Brother* and *Popstars* were dissimilar shows but they produced the same kind of celebrities – the kind who reside in the pages of *Heat* and are slagged behind their backs on Popbitch, a gossip website to which I was addicted. But neither earlier TV programme carried the same weight in the public imagination as *Pop Idol*. Nor did I feel the same way about them. The show felt like the last word in modern entertainment, or even something new – its success certainly encouraged more shows like it, like *Pop Rivals* and *Fame Academy* in the autumn of 2002.

I watched *Popstars* with a mixture of delight and self-disgust. I watched *Big Brother* with the furtive glee of a voyeur and a degree of concomitant shame. I read *Heat* in the bath every week until my toes started to shrivel, and wanted to drown myself for doing so.

I loved *Pop Idol*. I loved *Pop Idol* like I'd loved my first pop idol. It grew to be a bit embarrassing. *Pop Idol* was glitzy and glam and as cheesy as a stuffed pizza crust. It could never really be called a cool show. When I told people that I feasted at this table of light entertainment – on the sofa in front of the telly (if not eating a takeaway) – half of them assumed I must be watching with half a raised eyebrow and applauding the contestants ironically. But that was not the case.

Fortunately, the other half just wanted to gossip

about how much they hated Darius. So perhaps I wasn't alone. Still, my love for the show bothered me.

It's normally the sort of claim I make late at night in a spirit of relaxed enthusiasm, but I've always had impeccable taste in music. The pop industry was founded in 1952 in this country when that November the fledgling *NME* published the first pop charts. I like to think that on my CD shelves (meticulously arranged alphabetically within genre) there's a perfect selection of records from the fifty years that followed. You won't find any Kylie Minogue or Westlife there.

The first single I bought was Adam and the Ants' 'Stand And Deliver' in 1981, when I was ten. I guess it must have been the make-up – that slash of white paint across the bridge of Adam's nose – and the business of dressing up as a dandy highwayman which first appealed. But soon I started checking out his back catalogue and the sex and fetishistic-themed *Dirk Wears White Sox*. From that point on I was proper pop fan: a proper kind of snob.

At school, when everyone else was into the Human League, I didn't just have *Dare*, I had *Being Boiled*. When everyone else was into metal and groups like Twisted Sister – an act with the sound of some nu metal idiots and the looks of Christina Aguilera – I was giving props to Public Enemy. And I had turned into an indie kid. 'Indie' is the great unchronicled – unfêted even – chapter in the history of rock. While everyone else was listening to Stock, Aitken and Waterman, I was in my bedroom, trying to work out the significance of the obscene pictograms on a Butthole Surfers album because they functioned as title tracks. 'Indie' bore its poor relationship with mainstream culture as a badge of pride.

Later, my tastes broadened, and I started checking out jazz, and blues and folk. Good God – I even bought some classical music. In time, I could see that I might give up on pop itself completely. When *Pop Idol* started I was in the middle of a big Bob Dylan fix, bingeing on the more obscure stuff, including the Christian and mid-nineties albums. Yet watching *Pop Idol*, I realised I'd been missing something along the way.

The last time the media looked to have run with a story like *Pop Idol* was during Britpop. It had been a time which seemed to offer a way back into pop for me. I can clearly remember playing a pre-release cassette of the first Oasis album to my best friend Ken on the way to a gig. Despite my barmy enthusiasm, he didn't get it. Six months later everyone did. When Blur and Oasis announced they were releasing new singles on the same day in August 1995, it made *News at Ten*.

Yet both bands were already treading water artistically – 'Country House' and 'Roll With It' weren't a patch on their earlier singles. The scene soon soured into exactly the celebrity culture we know today. By 2002 you had to ask where it had all gone wrong. Damon Albarn still had some tabloid cachet but Blur had stopped writing songs about Mr Robinson doing the tango at a quango. Oasis seemed more content than ever to play to the lowest common denominator and churned out meat-and-potatoes anthems to set to footage of Brazil beating England.

By this time, Liam Gallagher from the group was dating pop starlet Nicole Appleton and there was news that they were fans of *Pop Idol*. According to 'a source close to the pair' on the Internet site Yahoo! Music, the couple even argued furiously over who should win the show. As a picture of domestic bliss, it was hardly a John and Yoko bed-in, but to my gratification Liam was apparently keen on Darius and Will. Not Gareth.

Celebrities were everywhere. In 1812, Lord Byron published *Childe Harold's Pilgrimage* and 'awoke to find myself famous'. He is regarded as the first modern celebrity. But since that time the criteria for inclusion in the club have changed. It didn't take talent for the people who passed through the *Big Brother* household to find themselves splashed across the tabloids and celebrity magazines and interviewed on Graham Norton's show. This was the era of the Lottery, after all, when 'It could be you . . .'. Celebrity wasn't something strived for and earned. Celebrity came ready-made on a drinks mat at the Met Bar.

The gospel of this culture was *Heat*, which sold itself with the slogan 'the higher the IQ, the greater the need for gossip'. In 2002 it became the fastest-growing magazine in Europe, selling half a million copies every week. Its favourite cover stars were contestants from *Big Brother* or the kids from *Popstars* – or *Pop Idol*. *Popstars* was the nightmare that haunted the dreams of the makers of *Pop Idol*. This was a reality TV series which followed the making of a band through a series of auditions for its members. It had finished a year almost to the day before *Pop Idol* reached its climax, but in that week before the final there was still plenty of news about the band *Popstars* had produced. Hear'Say looked to be in mortal trouble. Despite enjoying the fastest-selling debut single of all time, and two subsequent number ones, the group had already released a second album which had flopped like a dipsoid, and founder member Kym Marsh walked out. On the Tuesday of the final *Pop Idol* week, the four remaining members of the band held open auditions to find Kym's replacement. Most papers – tabloid and broadsheet – sent young writers along to try to get picked. On Wednesday, the *Sun* led its front page with 'Hear'Say fix storm'. The band's new addition was a dancer who knew the band and had already worked with them. Their stunt had backfired horribly.

What of our new – semi-official – pop idol? On 25 February, Will Young released 'Evergreen'/'Anything Is Possible'. It became the fastest-selling single of all time, beating Band Aid's 'Do They Know It's Christmas', registering 1,108,659 sales in that week alone. The Band Aid disc, made eighteen years earlier in aid of famine victims in Africa, featured the cream of the British recording industry at the time – it was a warm-up for Live Aid. Will's record was made because he won a TV talent search show – and six months previously he was completely unknown.

Two weeks after that, Gareth put out his debut,

'Unchained Melody'. It also sold a million.

Yet I own both those singles. (OK. Someone sent me Gareth's as a joke.) And perhaps the most surprising thing I felt after finishing my journey through *Pop Idol* was that I might be falling back in love with pop music again.

I suggested this to Nicki Chapman when I met her when all the pop idols then inevitably went on tour after the series. For my sins, I had volunteered to review the show for the *Daily Telegraph*.

'You know,' Nicki said, 'older people always say that. No disrespect.' For the record: I am thirty-one. Chapman slightly older. 'They say: "It isn't really my kind of thing . . . but . . ."! It's like they're trying to dig themselves out of it. Ha ha ha!'

Then suddenly she became deathly serious. 'There's nothing wrong with pop music.'

But surely this couldn't be true! How could I like Dylan *and* Will Young?

In fact, what I really wanted to know wasn't why I wanted Will to win *Pop Idol* so badly. It was why I loved *Pop Idol* so madly.

After *Pop Idol* finished on TV, Liam Gallagher actually changed his tune. Listening to him, I thought perhaps he was right. My nagging doubts were articulated perfectly.

'People voting for their fookin' favourite bands is a load of wank,' he opined in an interview with the *NME*. 'It's a con. It either happens or it don't. That show is like diarrhoea. It's like sitting on the toilet all day and then [grimaces] something comes out. Then before you know it, there's a fookin' flood. You ought to see my TV, it's covered in spit 'cos I got that close to it going [mimes head an inch from the screen, incandescent with fury as Will croons 'Evergreen'], YOU . . . FUCKING . . . CUNT!'

2

POP IN CRISIS AND THE PROBLEM WITH HEAR'SAY

'I'm not knocking the music, but it's like packets of cereal' – Sir Elton John

In its fiftieth year, the British pop industry looked outwardly healthy. Despite a slowdown in the rest of the world, there was growth of 5.3 per cent by value in 2001. To the delight of a government that had gone out of its way to look groovy, the business was worth the best part of £4 billion. But all the statistics in the world couldn't disguise the truth: British music sucked a big one. Ajax Scott, editor of trade bible *Music Week*, told me: 'The industry is at a crossroads.'

If you wanted the good news, much of the growth was driven by British artists, with Dido, Robbie Williams, David Gray, the Stereophonics, Gabrielle, Steps and Travis heading the list of the best-selling artists of 2001. OK. But even the most cursory examination revealed that the business was desperately sick. Sales were up but the costs of making and marketing albums had sky-rocketed. Typically it took £1.5 million to launch a new act, which meant selling half a million copies of an album to break even. Very few new bands were achieving long-term success. Sure-fire hits were failing to sell. Real profits were almost certainly down. Single sales fell below the 60 million unit mark for the first time since 1993.

'Pop groups aren't really doing pop music at all,' reckoned Pet Shop Boy and former *Smash Hits* journalist Neil Tennant. 'They're doing some weird kind of show-businessy thing, which is really anodyne and pre-Beatles in its inspiration.' There was an idea.

'There is no darkness in Steps. The only darkness within that whole phenomenon is the sheer ambition in it, which has a cruel quality about it. Calculating, like Boyzone. It's an astonishingly calculated thing.'

At least we weren't alone in our plight. Sales fell globally in 2001, the market down 5 per cent in value. British acts weren't selling in America, but it wasn't as if their industry had prospered either. The problem of consumers burning CDs and illegally downloading music from the Internet was far more pronounced in the States and in Asia than here, and a number of home-grown artists such as Courtney Love were waging war against their record companies. Even Michael Jackson, the epitome of pop whoredom, attacked Sony when they claimed he owed them something like $200 million of studio time and promotion costs. As Val Azzoli, co-chairman of Atlantic Records, said: 'If the industry doesn't change the way we do business, we're going to go bankrupt.'

'Nowadays record companies want the quick buck from the Backstreet Boys, N'Sync, Britney Spears, S Club 7 and Steps,' said Sir Elton John. 'I'm not knocking the music, but it's like packets of cereal. There are too many of them, too many of them are average and mediocre, and I think it damages real people's chances, real talent, of getting airplay.'

There was a perception that the industry had lost touch with its roots. In his history of the Warner Music Group, former Warner Bros executive Stan Cornyn wrote: 'What we had accomplished in '69 we had forgotten in '99 . . . When money changed from being a wondrous shower and became ruler over all, everything suffered. Swarms of suits had, in the end, endorsed greed over boogie.'

Spark a fat one, dude! But even if those words conjure an image of a bunch of hippies issuing discs when the lunar cycle gives the OK, the analysis held some truth. It's easy to grow misty-eyed at the thought, but record companies were once owned by people who knew something about music and could spot a hit record from a country mile. If their hunch proved wrong, they only had themselves to blame. Men such as Ahmet Ertegun at Atlantic, Berry Gordy at Tamla-Motown and Chris Blackwell at Island mostly got it right.

What's more, they weren't just faceless bureaucrats – and if the business they founded was run in hell-raising seat-of-the-pants fashion, that was part of the point. As a guide on *How to Make It in the Music Business* says: 'the whole shooting match is as fickle, manipulative, unpredictable and fascinating as pop music itself. The music business is not for those who crave safety and security in their career. The only certainty is that anything can and normally does happen.' Ker-ay-zee . . .

Decisions now, however, were made by committee and acts were dropped and signed according to the diktats of the quarterly balance sheet. It seemed as if the music industry was just a kink in the gut of a well-lunched businessman.

In the early nineties, a small number of global conglomerates had consumed their smaller rivals so that by the start of the next decade five companies and their myriad subsidiaries controlled 80 per cent of the music industry in Europe. Universal, a constituent part of the French conglomerate Vivendi, whose main business was in mobile phones and water purification, led the field with a 23.9 per cent market share. EMI followed with 14.4 per cent, then Warner Music with 12 per cent, Sony with 11.3 per cent, and BMG with 8.1 per cent. Warner Music was part of AOL Time Warner and BMG was part of the German media group Bertelsmann.

The whole entertainment division of BMG accounted for 30.1 per cent of its turnover, with book publishing responsible for 30.8 per cent. The company employed a total of 65,000 people in forty-five countries.

The only company to remain independent was EMI – and what's more, it was British. It was there that the incipient crisis really bit. A decade of looking for acts capable of short-term high-volume sales had left the company strapped for cash. Confusion was reflected in that fact that Mariah Carey agreed a £38 million pay-off in January 2002, after her first album for the company under the terms of a new deal sold only two million copies. (It didn't help that the record was launched in the week of 11 September. Or that it was the music equivalent of hives.) Yet at the same time company bigwigs were trying to woo Robbie Williams with a contract worth £40 million.

In fact, at the start of 2002, chairman Alain Levy announced plans to restructure the company by pouring money into a couple of superstars and half a dozen biggish acts. This involved making 1,800 people redundant across the company and pruning the artists on the label. 'We have streamlined the artist roster, which I found fairly bloated,' he said. 'For example, we had forty-nine artists in Finland and I don't think there are forty-nine Finns who can sing.' (This went down like the arrival of a Panzer division at the gates of Helsinki among Finnish acts on EMI such as Bitch Alert and Ben's Diapers.) 'The creative part of the business seems to have become less important than ever. The majority of artists sell fewer copies of their second album than the first today. And there is a tendency to buy market share rather than create it, with indiscriminate spending on videos and advertising on TV.' No wonder a deal with BMG had been mooted at one stage.

Of course, the dangers of vertical integration could be exaggerated. When Clive Davis's fabled label Arista, which he'd built through use of his own two ears, became part of BMG, it didn't start marketing or selling its products in new or different ways. The big winner of the 2001 Grammys was one of Davis's artists, Alicia Keys. In early 2002, however, BMG president/CEO Rolf Schmidt-Holtz drew up plans for a radical reshaping of their global operations in an attempt to convince their parent company, Bertelsmann, that music was actually a viable business.

In uncertain economic times, it made sense for the employees of big corporations to chase the quick buck, in which case why bother investing money and energy in an act that might take two or three albums to develop? Successful artists whose sales had grown through word of mouth, such as Dido and David Gray, were exceptions. George Michael's publisher Dick Leahy had it right when he called it 'a fast food business'.

It is a worrying state of affairs for me. I grew up listening to the charts every early Sunday evening, but now find it hard to keep up with who is at number one. Bands you've never heard of shoot straight to the top, propelled by a huge marketing spend. One week later, they'll be gone. It's easy to slip into the language of a disabused agricultural labourer, but when I were a lad you watched songs slowly climb the charts and you knew who everyone was. Those days seem long gone now. I could just about tell the difference between Take That and their American rivals in the early nineties, but who can spot the difference between a group like Five and a band of cardboard cut-outs? Westlife enjoyed seven consecutive number ones and I couldn't name you one of them.

Frank Musker, chairman of the British Academy

of Songwriters, complained that 'A&R departments are no longer in the business of Artists and Repertoire. They have become high-level concept merchants who can't sell a new artist to their own record company unless there is a clear-cut marketing angle to be exploited. In the past the singer would make the record and then the record company would devise a marketing campaign around it. Now the tail is wagging the dog and the music is the last element of the equation to be put into place.'

> *'He drags the music business down whenever he rears his ugly head'* – Roger Daltrey

When Alain Levy said 'a lot of record companies are self-centred and focused on the executive being the star, not the artist', he could have been talking about BMG and Simon Cowell. The forty-three-year-old record executive was a product of the Home Counties whose father worked for EMI. He had been a teenager when punk exploded but was always more interested in disco and the chart hits of the day. 'I'll always stay in pop music,' he once said, 'because the only thing I understand is pop.' After joining the EMI post room in 1980, he soon found a job as a song plugger. In 1984 he formed the dance label Fanfare and had a couple of big hits with Sinitta's 'So Macho' and 'ToyBoy'. Later, when he hired Max Clifford as his personal publicist, there was news that he had had an affair with the dominating singer.

In 1991 Cowell joined the BMG subsidiary Arista. Noticing that the World Wide Wrestling Federation was pulling in audiences of more than 600,000, 'mostly totally fanatical kids', with a show on Sky TV, he signed the chief athletes, called them WWF Superstars, and landed a number-four hit with 'Slam Jam'. But, despite thirty-two subsequent Top 40 hits of a similar nature, our smooth Lothario then fell out with the label's hierarchy, after announcing plans to sign the Go Go Power Rangers, a TV cartoon band, and Zig and Zag, two TV puppets. 'The scorn that was directed to me . . . was indescribable,' he would later reminisce.

Yet Cowell glided on and, newly ensconced at RCA, another division of the German media group, things really took off. 'He thinks differently to any other A&R man I have ever come across,' Ged Doherty, the head of BMG's music division, later recalled. 'He doesn't beat around the bush. And he doesn't give a monkey's about what people think.' That might be considered a fortunate attribute, given what he did next.

In 1995, Cowell launched Robson Green and Jerome Flynn, stars of hit ITV series *Soldier Soldier*, as recording artists. He'd already trawled the karaoke bars of Blackpool to find out which songs went down best with the kind of people who might like these rough-hewn heart-throbs. By the end of the year, the two thespians were million-sellers, following the success of their chart-topping cover of 'Unchained Melody' and subsequent album. It was around this time that Cowell persuaded BMG to lift the cap off his bonus in exchange for royalties. 'That's when I started making serious money.' Future hits with acts such as Bob The Builder, whose 'Can We Fix It' was the best-selling single of 2000, followed.

It was easy to see why Cowell later attracted the ire of rock critics. He told the *Daily Telegraph*'s Neil McCormick, 'I would rather have a Westlife than a David Gray because at least with Westlife you have a degree of control over their career, rather than hoping he hits the right note at the right time and gives you another "Babylon".' That couldn't be right. Westlife are dreadful. Robson & Jerome are to singing what Kylie Minogue is to Fat Club. Bob The Builder is maybe only sort of OK. (In our household, we've always been big fans of Bob.)

Elsewhere Cowell said the pop industry was 'no different from the film business. Someone had to make the decision to cast Leonardo di Caprio in *Titanic*. It is a business choice. It's the same thing about putting a band together. The idea that a band can only be credible when they find each other is ludicrous.' The comparison with Hollywood was apt: both were big fans of the High Concept production. (*Armageddon* – one of my favourite movies, though I concede that it doesn't stand up to second viewing – demonstrates producer Jerry Bruckheimer's thinking perfectly: big rock heads towards Earth; Bruce Willis blows it up; roll credits.) You could understand where someone like Roger Daltrey, the trout-farming front man of The Who, was coming from when he said Cowell 'drags the music business down whenever he rears his ugly head'.

'Pop stars today have no longevity,' he continued. 'Rock'n'roll is not about singing perfect notes or being a showbiz personality. It's about the anger and the angst, man.'

Cowell enjoyed his biggest success with Westlife – they earned about £11 million with their first string of hits. Some of the band's boys were quite keen on rock rather than the lightweight R&B and pop they sang, but all understood the nature of their pact. 'With a product like Westlife, you've got to play it safe,' said Mark. And they worked hard for their success. Shane, who studied to be an accountant before the band took off, observed, 'I thought it would be driving your Ferraris all over the place, doing *Top of the Pops* once every three months and relaxing for the rest of it in a big house. But it's literally 24/7. It's not an easy job.'

Yet even hard work and knowing your place didn't guarantee success. Simon Cowell did have his fair share of failures with the bands he signed. In the late nineties, the majors tried to launch a number of girl groups. New big-budget acts such as Precious at EMI:Chrysalis and Thunderbugs at Sony bombed. Cowell's Girl Thing were billed as the next Spice Girls. They sold more like that Two Fat Ladies drum-and-bass album.

I can recommend a visit to the official Girl Thing website. It looks a lavishly expensive production, but when you start exploring there's pitifully little to see. Click on the press section and there's a solitary picture of the girls on the cover of *Smash Hits* in May 2000. Click on the news archive and there are only three items. One of them is the story of how two of the five girls went to see Robbie Williams in concert. Despite backstage passes, the pair went home robbed of the experience of meeting him. They had to drive back from Manchester to London and they didn't get to sleep until 3 a.m. before getting up four hours later to appear on the children's TV show *Live and Kicking*. And that's the anecdote.

The third and final news item is dated December 2000. The girls have gone. That website floats in the ether, a very modern memorial to the transient life of pop stars.

In 2000, sales of records specifically categorised as 'pop' fell to less than 40 per cent of the market for the first time in three years. Simon Cowell said pop was in 'the most boring period we've gone through'.

No one was quite sure what to do next. But then in the music industry, as screenwriter William Goldman said of Hollywood, 'nobody knows anything'.

> *'What was important was the recording side of things, but we'd be worrying because only one car had turned up and it didn't have blacked-out windows'* – Myleene Klass

When Nigel Lythgoe, London Weekend Television's head of entertainment, saw a TV show called *Popstars* in Australia in early 2000, he thought it would be perfect for Britain. But the show depended on finding someone in the music industry to play with him. The response he received was lukewarm, until Universal came into play.

Popstars reached its climax on 3 February 2001, when the five kids picked to be in the band were revealed through the programme to the public. Twelve million people watched the show that night.

The cameras continued to follow Danny, Kym, Myleene, Suzanne and Noel for the next six weeks, leading up to the release of their first single, 'Pure And Simple'. It stormed to number one as the fastest-selling debut in history. With twenty-three weeks of prime-time media exposure and that success, how could the band possibly fail? Even the trendies seemed to like them, with *The Face* magazine putting them on their April cover, dressing the five young lab mice in Helmut Lang and Dries Van Noten.

Yet no one predicted *Popstars*' success and no one seemed prepared for Hear'Say's triumph. Polydor, the Universal subsidiary to which they signed, were left with just one strategy: sell, sell, sell. The band rushed into making two albums in the space of six months. I've got the first one at home. I can honestly say that I've played it just the once. I don't believe that anyone with a pair of ears has sat through the second. It peaked at number 23 in the charts in December 2001. The band had meanwhile squeezed a tour in, playing thirty-six gigs across Britain in thirty days. Tabloid rumours of arguments within the band were already circulating.

It wasn't surprising. When the famous five won the show, they didn't even have a manager. Myleene complained: 'What was important was the recording side of things, but we'd be worrying because only one car had turned up and it didn't have blacked-out windows. Most of this job is dealing with people. It's ten per cent music, ninety per cent politics, dealing with producers, the record company, making sure everyone's happy.' Noel told *The Face*: 'We've been shot to this fame, and I still feel like a waiter. To tell you the truth, I'm really scared.' And even in this age of instant celebrity, Hear'Say's stratospheric rise was proving too much for its members to take. Nicki Chapman said, 'this band are doing in three months what The Spice Girls did in three years'. Follow that same compressed timescale: Hear'Say were heading for meltdown.

The son of a Birkenhead docker, Nigel Lythgoe had always been interested in show business and auditioned for a talent competition at the age of eleven before his father, horrified at the thought of his boy joining a nancy-boy profession, asked that he abandon his dreams. By the age of twenty-one, however, he was choreographing BBC dance troupe The Young Generation. He went on to work with Morecambe and Wise and The Muppets before moving into production.

At LWT, Lythgoe masterminded dozens of shows, including *Blind Date* and *Kids Say the Funniest Things*. A friend to stars like Cilla and Barrymore, he also groomed a new generation of presenters, including Davina McCall, presenter of *Big Brother*, and Ulrika

Jonsson, former girlfriend of the England football manager. But Lythgoe really made his name with early-nineties series such as *Gladiators*, which took Saturday night TV to a new level (whether high or low). (Butch men and women try and biff each other with outsized cotton buds.)

Not everything was so rosy. A *Gladiators/Holiday on Ice* hybrid called *Ice Warriors* flopped (prompting the quip 'I didn't take ice in my whisky for six months afterwards'), while *Survivor*, an expensive American series that Lythgoe imported here, never lived up to its hype. Billed as the ultimate TV reality show – it put a bunch of telegenic people on an island in the South Pacific and got them to vote each other off following a series of tests – it had proved the TV hit of the year in the States. To British viewers it felt like a fancy-dan version of *It's a Knock Out*. There was certainly nothing real about any of it.

Lythgoe later regretted the way it was hyped, saying the show was sold very badly to the British public. 'We had this "reality" side to it, and I don't like the term "reality TV" at the best of times, because as soon as you point a camera at someone, reality flies out the window. It was a game show. That was it. There was no reality, in the sense that there was no way I was going to let anyone die out there. It's really bad for press when people die on your show.'

Popstars was actually equally fake. Hear'Say were created to fulfil a specific brief, and its members assiduously trained in the real business of being a modern pop star: how to dance, what to wear, how to deal with the press. They could sing all right, but their talent seemed a negligible part of the equation. In fact, Hear'Say weren't just styled and produced to within an inch of their lives, they were forced to live together for the sake of the TV cameras, as if this were The Monkees all over again. The band members hated it, with Danny complaining that: 'the *Popstars* people wanted a few fireworks and fall-outs'. There were a number of leaks to the press coming from the house, for which Lythgoe, also a judge on the show, blamed Suzanne. According to Noel, the stories 'weren't coming from any of us, but they had to make good telly'.

Each member of the band was typecast. 'They definitely placed us where they wanted to place us,' Kym said of the powers that be. 'I think they made Suzy the cutie, the little girl who didn't say boo to a goose, and in actual fact Suzy has a temper. Hehehe! Don't be fooled by her exterior. But they didn't show that side.'

So the *Popstars* kids were actors – not artists – and they didn't even believe their lines. 'Being untouchable?' Suzy said. 'I can see how other pop stars are. But us as pop stars? No. People know us as normal people – people come up to us, fans, and say, "All right, Suzanne, how's your throat this week?"'

'What about Danny's one?' Myleene asked of one incident. '"You used to be a cleaner? I'll show you how to clean a toilet!" Who'd come up to Catherine Zeta-Jones and say that?'

Beyond that first record-breaking single, Hear'Say

were never going to appeal to people like me who already felt they didn't like contemporary pop. The only difference between this lot and their peers was that the members of the group were more easily recognisable to the public than the blokes in Blue or Westlife, thanks to months of prime-time television exposure. But Hear'Say turned out to be like every other contemporary pop act. The whole process confirmed the public's worst fears about the pop business. It was a top-down operation in which the kids had little say in how they were portrayed. In fact, in this instance, the record company didn't even have full control over the band. The Granada media group, the company behind *Popstars*, had wanted a stake in the sales of 'Pure And Simple' before the Independent Television Committee barred them. But they took a stake in some of Hear'Say's future profits.

Eventually, tempers within the band frayed to the point at which Kym stormed out. She had said, 'I don't want to live my life in the magazines, I want a private life,' but before news broke of her departure she had cannily negotiated a £300,000 deal with *OK!* magazine to cover her wedding to *EastEnders* star Jack Ryder. She had done well for herself.

When the band hired Johnny Shentall to replace her, the outlook was bleak. ITV2 screened a six-part documentary following the audition process, presumably out of some sense of loyalty to the band. The series featured the reviews editor of the *NME,* someone whose brief you might have thought would involve flobbing on bands like this, offering heartfelt advice like: 'They need to come out with something really dancey to remind us why Hear'Say were so exciting in the first place.' A new tour scheduled for September 2002 was cancelled.

Right from the start other pop acts had been sniping at the band. Before her departure, Kym had observed: 'What they didn't like is that we lifted the lid on the whole thing and people saw that you are just like Joe from down the road . . . Other pop bands desperately want to say we're the most manufactured band ever but we were only put together in the same way Steps or Five were. They still went to auditions, but it was on a much smaller scale.' Later she singled out Jay from Five for special mention. 'Everything I've read lately has got [him] saying we're a bunch of wankers . . . He's going on how their music is much more real than ours. It's pop music! You are singing pop music! He's not singing fucking Pavarotti!' In time, it all turned rather nasty – even for someone who normally takes pleasure in these kind of spats. I guess when it all went sour it felt bad, because the sales for 'Pure And Simple' had probably fooled the kids into thinking that we really did care for them. Instead we simply used them. The problem with *Popstars* was that it made great telly but a rubbish group.

There were signs of brightness in the pop arena – when it was done right, it *could* be done with great success. Cowell hit lucky with Westlife – in fact, he's had an unerring ear for the lowest common denominator throughout his career. S Club 7 were another group who sold googols, and they seemed to epitomise the virtues of manufactured pop. And a third was Steps, who didn't enjoy the same public profile as Simon Fuller's acts but made the best Abba records for twenty years. They were the work of Pete Waterman. He had been the man who ruined my teenage years. The really scary thing was, Cowell, Fuller and Waterman as well were hatching a plan together. That would be *Pop Idol*.

3

MY POP LIFE

'It was a return to the true pop tradition of screaming youth' – Adam Ant

I bought 'Stand And Deliver' from WH Smith's on Cornmarket in Oxford. The records section was towards the back of the shop, past the magazine racks with their comics and copies of *Shoot!* This was long before the advent of music super- and mega-stores. It was a seven-inch disc and probably cost me 90p; I'm not sure how much of a ten-year-old's pocket money that took in 1981.

Adam Ant was my first pop idol. And the Dandy Highwayman opened the door to the New Romantics and the likes of Culture Club and Duran Duran and is credited by rock historians with heralding a rebirth of pop in this country following the turmoil of punk. Weirdly, listening to that single again isn't a particularly rewarding experience, even if I can muster a fondness for the dah-diddly-quah-quah bits.

Before that happily, the first record I can remember hearing is 'Sugar Sugar' by The Archies, which was released two years before I was born in 1971, so I like to think that my parents were (still) possibly playing it while I was *in utero*. Didn't someone once say something about the potency of cheap music? I also have to thank Mum and Dad – who were married in '66 – for being Beatles and Dylan fans. I guess it was normal to be so back then. (My mum wore miniskirts all right and my dad's hair is quite long in some of those fading old colour photos, but I don't think they were quite part of Swinging London or fully fledged hippies.) Hearing *Abbey Road* and *Nashville Skyline* around the house when I was in nappies proved just as valuable as piano lessons or the expensive education that followed later in my life. I've always been quite careful about what sort of music we play when the kids are awake. Nothing wrong with more Beatles and Bob and a bit of Snoop Doggy Dogg, say I.

Meanwhile, my sister developed an interest in teen idols like Leif Garrett when she was ten or so. There was a story in one of the pre-teen mags she read like *Jackie* about how he'd burped when kissing a girl. Eurgh! Then there was *Grease*, whose soundtrack she bought, annotating the gatefold sleeve with scribbled scraps of paper with the song lyrics. I saw the movie two or three times – it was that and *Star Wars* for me – and perfected a brilliant imitation of the chicken-wing dance Travolta does on 'Summer Nights'. I'm sure the whole thing had an impact. Watching a clip (on the reissued soundtrack's CD-ROM) of the original Antipodean pop queen, Olivia Neutron-Bomb, singing 'You're The One That I Want' in her skintight black leathers proved an unaccountably moving experience recently.

Looking back, I wonder all the same whether I took the lyrics in. On 'Greased Lightning' Travolta sings something about getting lots of tit – and rhymes that with shit – and his veritable pussy wagon of a car makes the chicks 'cream'. I'm sure seven-year-olds didn't know about such things in 1978.

(A good footnote concerning *Grease*: the man who pushed to release 'You're The One That I Want' as a single in Britain was a young disc jockey from Coventry trying to make his way in the music business called Pete Waterman. The record later went to number one for nine weeks, selling close on two million copies.)

Thereafter I dimly recall a few records – my sister and cousins singing along to 'Figaro' by The Brotherhood of Man, 'YMCA' by The Village People (later memorably reprised on *Pop Idol*) and 'Video Killed The Radio Star' by The Buggles. This was all through punk and the New Wave, that followed, but none of that impacted on me much, even though by 1980 I knew enough to realise that The Jam and Dexys and Blondie were good, and The St Winifred's School Choir nothing other than evil. But then, for me, came Adam.

Stuart Goddard had always been interested in music and was a teenage fan of David Bowie, Roxy Music and Malcolm McLaren-managed proto-punks The New York Dolls. At Hornsey College of Art in north London (where his tutors included Roger Law, the future creator of *Spitting Image*), he developed a corresponding passion for the work of Andy Warhol and English Pop artists such as Allen Jones. This gave him a creative conception of pop music. 'From then on,' he later said, 'I designed everything myself. Adam and the Ants would become my graphic invention.'

While still in college he started playing bass with a group of fifties rock and roll revivalists called Bazooka Joe, and toyed with different stage names such as Eddie Riff. In November 1975 they played St Martin's College of Art, a notable gig because the support group playing their first-ever date was The Sex Pistols.

Inspired by Johnny Rotten's merry men, and a patron of Malcolm McLaren's shop on the King's Road, Let It Rock (later Sex), Eddie Riff mutated into Adam Ant and formed the Ants. The group's first single, 'Young Parisians', released by the ailing Decca in the summer of 1978, featured a sleeve designed and drawn by Adam himself. (I must have bought my copy – with the racy imagery – when it was reissued in 1982.) It promptly flopped.

Adam turned to McLaren, now recently separated from the Pistols, for advice. For a £1,000 fee, McLaren fed him with ideas about looks and music – turning him on to Burundi drumming – but ended up using the concepts himself, stealing Adam's band, sticking fifteen-year-old Annabella Lwin out front and calling them Bow Wow Wow. (You will, of course, remember that album sleeve ripping off Manet's *Déjeuner sur l'Herbe*.) Adam simply found a new collaborator in

Marco Pirroni and adoped his own Native American look. Their first single with a new band, 'Dog Eat Dog', entered the charts at number 50, climbed a week later to 37, then climbed again to number 19. After an appearance on *Top of the Pops*, the single rocketed to number four. These were the good old days.

On 21 February 1981, Adam and the Ants had a record five singles in the Top 75 at the same time. Later that month the band appeared at the Royal Variety Performance at the London Palladium. Adam was stunned to be asked to give an autograph to Princess Margaret. As The Buggles predicted, old radio stars were in trouble. Adam was one of the pioneers of the pop promo – which came in handy when MTV was launched in America that August. Even so, he had to talk his new label, CBS, into giving him the money to make the clip for his next single, 'Stand And Deliver', which is where I came in . . .

The video was directed by Mike Mansfield, a veteran of sixties TV rock programme *Ready Steady Go*, but it was Adam, who had also trained in film at art school, who came up with the concept and elaborate storyboard. The single went to number one for five weeks.

The promo for 'Prince Charming', which followed, was even more memorable. The record inaugurated yet another new look, which Adam patented through the Merchandizing Corporation of America, trying to enforce his legal control over every last sleeve, badge, T-shirt, poster or sticker bearing his face or name.

Adam recognised that popular music was all about belonging to a tribe or club – like the teddy boys or mods or hippies or punks – and so invented his own Ant Clan. From there it's not such a great leap to Simon Fuller's S Club project.

The singer's rise was mirrored by the rise of the pop and style press. *Smash Hits* was launched in 1979, followed by *The Face* in 1982 and *Number 1* the following year. In 1983 the four music weeklies – the *NME*, *Melody Maker*, *Sounds* and *Record Mirror* – sold little more than half the number they had in 1980. But the addition to news-stands of the new glossy magazines meant that there was nearly a 35 per cent increase in sales of major music titles over the course of three years.

There had been teenybopper mags before *Smash Hits*, like *Rave* in the sixties, but before the advent of new colour printing technologies it was hard to capture the bright allure of pop music. Nick Logan's publication soon became the house organ of the kiddier end of the New Romantic movement. (A development signalled by the graphic icon of the gossip columnist changing from a suited gent, a mod possibly, to a floppy-fringed smoothie in a *Miami Vice* outfit.) Logan followed it with *The Face* in 1982, which concentrated on music to begin with (featuring major interviews with Jerry Dammers, Paul Weller and David Bowie in its early issues), but slowly pioneered the concept of a lifestyle magazine. Pop was treated seriously, but so was pop culture, which included fashion, in particular, and film and art and so on. It was very big on scenes and teenage tribes. It was also perfect for the new pop scene.

Adam always ignored the *NME* and *Melody Maker*, who always slagged him off (though the long-deceased *Sounds* was kind on occasion), and went straight to these new publications. 'It was a return to the true pop tradition of screaming youth,' he later said of his success. 'And it was the pop papers. The most important thing really was the photographs.'

Adam still charged *Smash Hits* twice the going rate to reproduce the lyrics to his hits.

I bought 'Prince Charming' and the album of the same name that came out two months later. The album was a real piece of work, complete with gatefold sleeve (even if the centrefold picture of the band was oddly out of focus), but it only went to number two, kept off the top by Queen's *Greatest Hits* (which my sister bought, so we cancelled each other's votes in this chart election). Critical enthusiasm was also muted, which further upset Adam because to him it was a very serious record 'based on very classical, historic themes, like Commedia dell'arte of the 17th and 18th centuries'. And actually, I never cared for 'Prince Charming' much. At any age you recognise bollocks when you hear it.

With alarming speed, Adam then drifted off my pop map. Within three years he was treading the boards, taking the title role in a production of Joe Orton's *Entertaining Mr Sloane* at the Royal Exchange in

Manchester. It's funny, but at the time I had no idea. He did play Live Aid in 1985 but looked like an anachronism and indeed was the only artist on the bill whose sales went down after the concert.

'Whatever the rhetoric . . .' Bob Geldof

Did punk – and Adam was a punk – ever change the world? The authors of 'God Save The Queen' may have talked the talk in 1977 but last time I looked Her Majesty was celebrating her Golden Jubilee with a party at Buckingham Palace featuring the biggest names in pop (everyone from Sir Paul McCartney to William Young). McLaren and The Sex Pistols made monkeys of the record business (earning £75,000 for their six-day stint with A&M; ridiculing EMI on record) but the victory was pyrrhic. Former Boomtown Rat and Live Aid saint Bob Geldof, for one, recognised that criticising the Pistols at the time was akin to criticising Marx in a Politburo meeting, but that for all the anarchy in the UK the band still signed contracts, attended rehearsals, and wrote songs. 'Whatever the rhetoric, in the end being in a band was about hard work and demanded discipline.' As for being the Stones to the Pistols' Beatles, the most rebellious thing The Clash ever did was refuse to play *Top of the Pops*.

Punk was never a great commercial success either. *Never Mind The Bollocks* did make it to number one in November 1977, displacing Cliff Richard's *40*

Golden Greats, but it stayed there for only two weeks before losing out to *The Sound Of Bread* by Bread. Between 1976 and 1979 the band only made the Top 10 with four singles (compared to The Beatles' nine number ones between 1963 and 1966). It passed me by as a pop infant. The only safety pins I ever knew had been in my nappies.

Nonetheless, I grew up with a strong sense that the sixties and punk both saw some kind of pop cultural utopia, when the kids ran free. What joy it must have been to be alive in the spring, smoking dope in Hyde Park when Mick Jagger let those poor butterflies flap out of that box at that Stones gig or sniffing glue while avoiding the spray of phlegm at a Sham 69 gig!

So you don't have to negotiate the collected works of a pop theorist like Greil Marcus – life's too short, I promise – to realise that punk did have an effect. Even in the most nebulous sense, it perpetuated the romantic myth that things can be otherwise – *sous les pavés, la plage!*

Reflecting on punk at the time of its own silver jubilee, McLaren wrote that it demystified the culture, creating something truly authentic compared with the karaoke culture that we are held to enjoy today ('a life by proxy, liberated by hindsight, unencumbered by the messy process of creativity', according to Malc). Of course, the strange thing about this is that McLaren has always previously claimed that the Pistols were principally his creation, which imposes a top-down view of punk. Perhaps the great Svengali became a softie in old age. Certainly he felt 'confused' that the former Johnny Rotten had recently said he was never 'pro' or 'anti' monarchy and that while we've got a monarchical system it might as well 'work properly'. (Boo!)

The sad truth, in fact, is that, in the short term certainly, the DIY ethos of punk was perverted by Adam Ant to turn himself into a pop star. Those who didn't take the Carnaby Street tourist dollar soon followed. And perhaps that Utopia will remain but a pipe-dream.

Here's proof. Try looking at the best-selling singles of 1981 and identifying the punk tunes. The exercise proved what can only be described as a Proustian experience for me, with almost every song suggesting the very texture of life as I experienced it then.

1. 'Tainted Love' by Soft Cell
   Failing to teach my friend Rick Wold the words
2. 'Stand And Deliver' by Adam and the Ants
3. 'Prince Charming' by Adam and the Ants
4. 'This Ole House' by Shakin' Stevens
   Always despised him; still tried to imitate his dancing
5. 'Vienna' by Ultravox
   Unspeakably outraged that this masterpiece – whatever it was about – was kept off the top by 'Shaddap You Face' by novelty singer Joe Dolce

6. 'One Day In Your Life' by Michael Jackson
   No, sorry. No recollection of it
7. 'Making Your Mind Up' by Bucks Fizz
   Cheryl and the other one whipping off their skirts when they sang it in the Eurovision final
8. 'Shaddup You Face' by Joe Dolce
   Wanker
9. 'The Birdie Song' by Tweets
   Nice moment on Big Brother 3 when the contestants heard a blast of it, and started doing the dance round the room
10. 'You Drive Me Crazy' by Shakin' Stevens
11. 'Ghost Town' by The Specials
    Wow
12. 'Being With You' by Smokey Robinson
    Who? I had absolutely no idea who he was
13. 'It's My Party' by Dave Stewart and Barbara Gaskin
14. 'Woman' by John Lennon
    I was in the changing rooms at the Cowley baths after a school swimming lesson when someone told me he'd been killed (on 8 December 1980). Even then I knew it mattered
15. 'Happy Birthday' by Altered Images
    Always had a bit of a crush on Claire Grogan. Gregory's Girl: screen classic
16. '(Give Me Your Heart)' by Ottowan
    Disco classic
17. 'Stars on 45' by Star Sound

> *The history of pop on one seven-inch; who needs a CD library or fancy modern bastard bootleg mixes?*
> 18. 'Green Door' by Shakin' Stevens
> 19. 'Imagine' by John Lennon
> 20. 'Jealous Guy' by Roxy Music

(Even in the lower reaches of the Top 50 there are songs whose lyrics I can remember word for word, even though I haven't heard them for over twenty years. Am I alone in holding 'Do The Hucklebuck' by Coast to Coast close to my heart?)

There were still some acts who promised to shake things up a bit in punk's wake, like The Jam. 'I find politics the single most uninspiring, unemotional, insensitive activity on the planet,' Adam said. Paul Weller raged back, complaining to *Record Mirror* about 'this show-business crap, like Adam Ant wants to bring back. He just makes me puke.' His band had a quiet year in 1981 by their own standards (just two Top 10 hits) but scored four the next year, including two number ones. But at that point they split. And increasingly people took the piss out of Weller; and I never bought The Style Council's records.

The Specials were an extraordinary group – multi-racial, from the streets, brilliant songwriters and political as fuck. It seems extraordinary to me now that a song like 'Ghost Town' could ever get to number one, but for three weeks in July of '81 it did top the charts, just as riots engulfed Toxteth and Brixton. But the band split immediately after that success.

Fun Boy 3 were one result, who for all their political intent couldn't help but be regarded as a pop act, particularly when they duetted with Bananarama on 'It Ain't What You Do, It's The Way That You Do It'. The Specials had been signed to the independent 2-Tone; Fun Boy 3 went with the major label Chrysalis.

Otherwise, the next two years witnessed acts indebted to Adam flourish, including Spandau Ballet (a Chrysalis act), Duran Duran (EMI) and Culture Club (Virgin). I remember discussing Boy George in the school playground the day after witnessing him singing 'Do You Really Want To Hurt Me' on *Top of the Pops*, in September 1982. There was something fascinating about him – most obviously, I guess, the fact that he wore dresses and make-up. But the funny thing was how homely he seemed. And really, for all their girly looks, these mincers were entirely conventional, and terrifying products of their time. These acts weren't interested in anything other than the projection of their own image and so put the narcissistic ethos of Thatcherism on sale in the shops. There were elements of punk there, in the dandified anarchy of their dress, for one thing, but as a biography of Boy George and Culture Club put it, this really was Like Punk Never Happened. It was the start of the Me decades.

Of course, there have been pop acts who have tried to buck the system from within. Frankie Goes To Hollywood made good on McLaren's promise with

The Sex Pistols by selling millions of records with songs about gay sex and World War III. But it was easy to see through this lot. As pop academic Simon Frith wrote in the *Village Voice*: 'It's the smoothness of Frankie's success that unnerves me – it's hard to find anyone . . . who thinks that Frankie, or their records, are changing the way people understand their lives. They're a best-selling group without real fans, more like the Archies than The Sex Pistols. And this reflects they way they've made it – through marketing rather than live performance. Their energy is the energy of pop's sales team rather than its consumers – there are, presently, more TV pop shows than ever before, more knowing pop people in record company control, more competitors for the leisure pound.'

(And of course Frankie's success had very little to do with the pseudo-academic claims made on their behalf by their strategist, the journalist Paul Morley, and everything to do with the catchy tunes and slick production of Trevor Horn.)

There is plenty of irony here. Punk may not have changed the pop landscape. But did Adam? There's no doubt that the New Romantics were the big stars of their day, and I bought lots of the records (the first Duran album; a couple of Culture Club seven-inches), as well as some singles by others who followed them like the young Depeche Mode. But these weren't really pop's golden years.

Look at the sales figures. Record sales rose by 4.1 per cent and 4 per cent in 1981 and 1982, but once inflation is taken into account the real value of sales was at an all-time low. When full statistical records began in 1975, singles and albums were worth £770.6 million at 2000 prices. In 1982 that figure was £557.9 million.

The old punks just succeeded in dragging sales down to their own level. Adam Ant didn't save pop – he just killed rock's last hurrah. But there was room on the pop landscape for a figure far more sinister.

> 'I have never treated popular music as candyfloss. I've never treated it as life or death. I've treated it as a cultural item that needs some respect and understanding' – Pete Waterman

This is where Pete Waterman came in. The young producer had his first hit in October 1982 with Musical Youth's 'Pass The Dutchie', the work of a group of West Indian Brummies. In its first incarnation, the song was called 'Pass The Coochie', a reference to some kind of apparatus for smoking dope. The title was changed – though Waterman later said, 'to be honest, I never completely bought the cooking pot explanation' – and he added some percussion and keyboards. He was sitting at home watching the telly when he saw the headlines on *News at Ten*: 'Reggae Boys From Birmingham Have Number One Hit!' The single stayed at the top for three weeks. In the States, Musical Youth became the first black group to have their video played on MTV.

Waterman set up his own company, Pete Waterman Limited, against the advice of everyone in the business at the time. 'Everyone forgets that when I started PWL, people all told me I was a fucking idiot,' he told me when we met. '"You're a fucking idiot. Singles are dead." Yeah, *right*. I have sold since 1982 easily five hundred million singles.

'Some fucking death. Some singles.'

After that first hit, Waterman had a quiet year before meeting Mike Stock and Matt Aitken, two obscure young songwriters and studio hands. Their first record as a partnership, a disco number called 'The Upstroke', found fans in the most unlikely places – the first person ever to play a SAW track on the radio was John Peel. But the team needed to harness their talents to a sexier vehicle before they started having hits. Their first number one was Dead Or Alive's 'You Spin Me Round' (for which Waterman claims he nicked half the production ideas from Wagner's 'Ride of the Valkyries') with the extraordinary Pete Burns on vocals. That was perhaps a step too far.

The Stock, Aitken and Waterman team went on to be responsible for heinous crimes against music such as Mel and Kim and Rick Astley and that red-headed pixie from Liverpool, Sonia. Although the records were made with state-of-the-art equipment they displayed the aesthetic texture of a ghastly shiny eighties suit. Although the acts mouthed the words on the shoddy videos, they had less life than Max Headroom. Although some of them had principles, they kept them secreted in a closet bigger than Boy George's. There's a nice story in Waterman's wonderful autobiography about Siobhan from Bananarama refusing to sing the line 'Ain't life a bitch, you gotta keep on working till you strike it rich' on one song, complaining that it was 'capitalist'. Waterman ignored her and just employed the voices of the two other girls. Later, when Siobhan announces she is getting married to Dave Stewart and they hire a jumbo to take guests (including Bob Dylan) to the South of France, Waterman says to her: 'That's a bit gauche for a socialist, isn't it?' (She was perhaps more New Labour.)

Actually, I quite liked Mel and Kim (particularly those 'tay/tay/tay/tay/t-t/t-t/t-t-tay' bits) and the 'Nanas, but Kylie Minogue and Jason Donovan weren't even "real singers". *Neighbours* played big in our house, but I wouldn't be seen dead buying records by actors. Famously, Waterman had never really heard of Kylie when she turned up at the PWL studios in south London en route to the airport to catch a flight home to Australia in late 1987. Their success with 'I Should Be So Lucky' took the company to another level, and the team sold something like 40 million records in the next two years. Between March 1986 and October 1990, there was a single produced by Pete Waterman in the Top 100 every week. Kylie had ten Top 10 hits in that period, including four number ones, one of which was 'Especially For You', her nauseating duet with Jason. He had seven other Top 10s, and two solo number ones. That's more than

Bob Dylan in the course of his entire career (highest chart positions: 'Like A Rolling Stone', number four, 1965; 'Lay Lady Lay', number five, 1969). Footnote: one of the first albums Will Young ever bought was Kylie's first, with 'I Should Be So Lucky' on it.

Pete Waterman made my musical life at the time a misery. It was impossible to escape his records in their ubiquity. It was horrifying to think that pop could be rendered so lifeless. It was shocking to think that what glam attraction there was in the New Romantics had been boiled down to this insipid consommé. It was as if there was no romance and no life-affirming resonance left in my universe.

Pete Waterman is an extraordinary man. Born into an ordinary family in Coventry in 1947, amid post-war deprivation ('we had curtains, even if they were cardboard'), his uncle was the Wagner fan, while his sixteen-year-old cousin Jean introduced him to the joys of proto-rock and rollers like Johnnie Ray. He saw The Beatles play in front of a hundred people at the Coventry Matrix (for eight bob) in 1962, joined a couple of bands for a very short time (before realising he didn't have 'any genuine talent'), and started deejaying and running clubs. 'I've been part of pop culture since about '57, and I've seen pop culture change, and I've seen it change not for the better sometimes,' he told me. 'I would like to think, no matter what people think, that I still love the music, I still adore what I do. To me, I'm still the luckiest guy in the world. [To think that] I could leave school unable to read or write and become a multimillionaire . . . the money isn't important but the fact that I can sit down every week and still hear people singing my songs and love every moment of what I do, I think, is different . . .

'I can look back at what's almost a fifty-year career – there ain't anyone else who's done that. I've never become blasé. If I have a miss I get upset about it and then go and research it all over again. When somebody doesn't buy my record, I do physically look at it and say, "Why?"'

Waterman became a successful Northern Soul DJ and moved into making records, after following up a standing invitation to visit Philadelphia International, the studio of Kenny Gamble, Leon Huff and Tom Bell, in 1973. Like the great Motown in Detroit in the sixties, Philly Int. fabricated peerless modern soul, which at this point was slowly mutating into disco. Gamble, Huff and Bell productions such as 'Love Train' by The O'Jays and later 'Don't Leave Me This Way' by Harold Melvin and the Bluenotes were huge hits, and went down a storm with Waterman's clubbing clientele in provincial England. He stuck out like a sore thumb in Philly – the only white man at the studios, the butt of a Richard Pryor diatribe when the self-styled Crazy Nigger played a gig in town – but was awestruck the way in which the records were assembled like cars on a factory line.

But if all that sounds too predictable, the real thing that attracted Waterman to this sweatshop was not the business model. Rather, he loved the seriousness that the Philly International team brought to their music, the passion. In Britain at this time the pop charts were dominated by rackety glam acts such as Suzi Quatro and Sweet. 'Great music,' Waterman wrote in his book, 'but the acts were more important than the songs.' Good for him.

It was wonderful meeting my nemesis. It should have been in a dark alley at night (though I'm not sure I'd fancy myself). Instead the interview took place in an air-conditioned office at the PWL studios, which are so unassuming that I walked past the scruffy building twice before finding it. I can't say going there thrilled me like visiting Studio One in Kingston or Stax in Memphis might. But this was a real hit factory, and Waterman soon seduced me. It isn't that he has had a hand in more number ones than Lennon and McCartney, though that's an achievement that at least demands respect. It isn't that I have recanted and have been turned on to the joys of early SAW recordings in my middle youth through some kind of sense of perverted irony either. In the interests of research, I bought Kylie's *Greatest Hits* the other day (Amazon don't stock her first album, funnily enough), and it's *arsewipe*. It's the fact that Waterman is utterly hilarious, always right and more rock and roll than . . . well, at least Simon Cowell.

Listen to Pete to hear the real history of British pop. 'There hadn't been a phenomenon like Rick [Astley] before,' he writes in his autobiography, 'and some would say there hasn't been one like him since.' That's not a view you will find in *Mojo* magazine.

Listen to Pete, talking to me, on the art of writing pop songs: 'I have treated popular music very seriously all my life. Always. I have never treated it as candyfloss. I've never treated it as life or death. But I've treated it as a cultural item that needs some respect and understanding. I've never thought it's easy. In fact, I probably think it's the hardest thing ever.

'What makes the difference between "Moon, June, and Soon" and "Never Gonna Give You Up"? You have to rhyme but you don't have to rhyme; you have to have a melody that's simple but that's not simple; it has to be complicated but not complicated; it's light but dark; it's dark but light; it's fast but slow; it's loud but soft. Pop music is a contradiction in absolutely every part of its make-up. So when people say it's interesting, I say, "Go on . . ."'

Listen to Pete on what happened to my first pop idol: no matter how pretty he looked, 'people will only buy what they want to buy, it doesn't matter if it's on telly seven nights a week. If they don't like it, they don't buy it.'

So why did I like Adam? Waterman, funnily enough, had listened to 'Stand And Deliver' the other day too, and couldn't agree more with my harsh new verdict of it. There was good karma between us. 'Adam was a character. But it could have been Dennis The Menace you also loved.' So *that* was it.

And there is a final reason for me to thank Pete

Waterman. Without Kylie and company, there would have been no one against whom I could measure the qualities of the bands I learnt to love when I grew out of Adam. Looking for reasons to like some of the dodgier indie acts foisted on me by the inkie music papers, it helped that they stood in some kind of opposition to the manufactured dross emanating from Waterman's studios. And it was dross! Pop is all about tribalism, and for that to work, you need something to rail against.

The irony here was that PWL was actually an independent record company and SAW was an indie label. Each week the *NME* and *Melody Maker* used to publish the official charts and the indie charts, as if this list of movers and shakers was somehow more authentic. For me, it was one thing to comprehend the existence of SAW's records somewhere in the greater universe of pop, quite another to see the Antipodean chipmunk snuggling up to the Butthole Surfers in the column inches of my weekly fix of print.

> 'We spent most of the time doing cocaine in the toilets. We didn't spend much time thinking about the starving in Ethiopia' – Francis Rossi

Live Aid, which took place on 13 July 1985 with me sat in front of the telly all day, was the biggest event of my early pop life. Hey, it was supposed to be my generation's Woodstock. Was it arse. There were some New Romantic has-beens, like the Durannies and Adam, and eejits who'd emerged in their wake like Nik Kershaw and The Thompson Twins. But mostly this was an occasion to demonstrate that the old behemoths of rock which punk had set out to destroy were still standing. The bill included gods of the sixties – McCartney, Dylan and Keef and Ronnie from the Stones making tits of themselves, and The Who, who reformed for the occasion at Wembley. Acts like Crosby, Stills and Nash, whom I'd never heard of at the time, took the stage at JFK Stadium in Philadelphia. But younger bands like U2 seized the opportunity too to make a name for themselves and make it clear that they belonged in such company. The whole thing was wrapped up in a blanket of smugness. 'What impresses me about today,' said Daryl Hall of Hall & Oates, 'is that people who have a certain amount of sensitivity and artistic tendencies can be heard, and their music can make a difference.' Twat.

The event offered these stars an opportunity to engage with the wider world – to make a statement about the nature of modern rock – but the extent of their commitment to the cause was at best questionable. 'We spent most of the time doing cocaine in the toilets,' said Francis Rossi of Status Quo, who opened the Wembley show with an amazingly energised performance of 'Rockin' All Over The World'. 'We didn't spend much time thinking about the starving in Ethiopia.'

> *'That was a great marketing experience. A very powerful experience'* – Al Teller

Live Aid really marked the corporate take-over of mainstream rock music. It was a development signalled earlier by the rise of Bruce Springsteen, who had emerged as the biggest act on Earth in the slipstream of Johnny Rotten's gob. The New Jersey singer was managed by Jon Landau, who had taken over control of the MC5 from their radical mentor John Sinclair at the end of the sixties, and overseen their dissipation. Under Landau's guidance, The Boss sold several trillion copies of *Born In The USA* on its release in 1984, despite it being an overblown piece of hokum masquerading as social critique. (Or perhaps because it was.) This was the point at which rock became just as much of a commercial entity as kiddie pop.

Springsteen's chief selling-point was that he looked like a man of the people and was sensational in concert with his band. Well, rock of course is dependent on establishing a deep and meaningful relationship between act and listener (even the fact that you play rock music by hammering strings against a block of wood suggests a certain physical immediacy and intimacy), and live performance is a great way to form that relationship. CBS carefully nurtured Springsteen's blue-collar image and, with his blessing, sent him out on the road again and again and again and again.

After the campaign for *Born In The USA* had finally finished, CBS records' senior vice president and general manager Al Teller reflected: 'That was a great marketing experience. A very powerful experience.' E Street organist Danny Federici spoke to writer Fred Goodman from a very different point of view. 'We started out as a band, which turned into a super, giant corporate money-making machine.'

The arrival of the CD in the early eighties further strengthened that bond between act and fans, as ageing listeners began to fill in missing chapters from the history of rock music, as it was assiduously shuffled into place. Corporate lapdogs like Dire Straits exploited the arrival of the new format by making the sort of polished rock that sounded *great* on new equipment (just as The Eagles had heralded the arrival of FM radio in America in the early seventies). The *NME* punned in their review of the mega-selling *Brothers In Arms* that it was for 'compact dickheads only'. The album contained 'Money For Nothing', a sly dig at MTV that promptly became a rallying cry for the new station ('I want my MTV!'). The groundbreaking video for the song won the Best Video and Best Group Video categories at the third annual MTV Music Awards in 1983. In the two years since its launch, the station's audience had grown in America from 2.1 to 16.2 million. MTV was perfect for the music industry: TV with no programming, only advertising.

This was all part of a process which robbed

mainstream rock in the eighties of all its vitality. It wasn't pretty to see.

Yet I have a horrible confession to make: I think I bought *Brothers In Arms*. I can't be sure. Perhaps it was my sister. But it did live in our household.

Thankfully, within a couple of years I'd seen the error of my ways. I know at that point I binned the record, which seemed almost sacriligious, but this was a mercy killing. Up until that point I had been fairly catholic in my tastes, willing to try out anything, buying records because, I guess, I liked the tune.

Now, however, was the time to draw up battle lines.

'For all the fucked-up children of the world . . .' –
Spacemen 3 T-shirt slogan

By the time Pete Waterman was in his pomp I'd long since fallen in love with bands like The Pixies, My Bloody Valentine, Dinosaur Jr, Spacemen 3, and The Butthole Surfers . . . How lucky we were! I still have my Buttholes T-shirt with a lurid green print of a pig being given an injection and the slogan 'Better living through chemistry' and a Spacemen one with the slogan 'For all the fucked-up children of the world, we give you Spacemen 3'. Cool. But none of these rock bands ever made much impact on the outside world. They were far less visible than the New Romantics. They would never be on MTV, like Dire Straits, or would never have a TV series to themselves.

There are no two ways about it: I became an indie kid. If pop is all about dressing up, there wouldn't really be a place on the fashion parade with the teddy boys or mods or even the hippies or punks for me in the mid-eighties. I was a scruffy-haired, slouching, middle-class kid in a floppy T-shirt, but no strong tribal style. As for ideology, we were average. As for energy, distinctly average. And as for the music . . . were you ever at a Ride or Slowdive gig? It seemed as if my generation had been handed the short straw.

I remember my sister and her friends taking the piss out of me when they were still in their Siouxsie phase and I was wearing a skinny Jesus and Mary Chain T-shirt. This must have been in 1985, when the Reid brothers, augmented by the young Bobby Gillespie clattering the drums, charted with three singles (peaking at 47, 55 and 45 respectively). They specialised in screeching frenzies of feedback married to the harmonic lustre of what I would only later recognise as the sound of the early Beach Boys. It was East Kilbride meets West Hawthorne, Los Angeles. Rockin'.

The JAMC pointed the way backwards, however, for a host of bands like The Pastels and The Bodines, who specialised in sub-Beatlesy and sub-Byrds jingle-jangle fartiness, and looked embarrassed to be caught at it. Bobby Gillespie's first band of his own, Primal Scream, could be included among that sorry bunch. It was a sound devoid of any musical spark, bleached of any sexual or political urgings, heavily reliant on the imagery of the Beach Boys' rivals and total opposites on the East Coast of the States in the sixties, The Velvet Underground. Of course, I promptly discovered their oeuvre for myself, along with bands like The New York Dolls and MC5 – and Iggy, of course, Detroit's other great musical export with Motown. To compare with these figures of Dionysian excess, we had McCarthy and The Field Mice.

And worse was yet to come. Slowdive, Chapterhouse, Ride and Lush were whey-faced wallflowers from the Home Counties – hilariously, there was talk of a Thames Valley Scene at one point – who exhibited the personality of a garden centre. This lot even earned their own sub-genre: shoe-gazing.

For me, there was a horrible sense of recognition about it all, because these people could have been at school with me in Oxford. There were people I knew who sort of knew the lippy one out of Ride. It could have been me up there. Perhaps that's why I hated them with a particular vengeance – I knew that I would make a crap rock star. I knew the Thames Valley wasn't buzzin'. It all seemed too depressing.

But any generic label for a style of music inevitably flatters the worst while belittling the best. Punk had The Sex Pistols but also Slaughter and the Dogs. We had Slowdive but My Bloody Valentine too. My Bloody Valentine boasted not of taking drugs but of going without sleep for weeks on end, and made the kind of fuzzy head-music of your dreams. They were also a compelling live act. I saw them in front of about a hundred people at Oxford Poly around 1988, and pressed my head against the speaker stack throughout the epic 'You Made Me Realise', which featured a three-day burst of feedback, losing myself in the strange harmonies that emerged from the blizzard of white noise. I couldn't hear properly for about a month afterwards. Years later I read an article in *Mojo* about the loudest rock bands of all time, which rated MBV in the top five. Never mind.

Then there was Spacemen 3, who could out-drone-rock anyone – they could out-Loop Loop! – but also did beautiful, meditative numbers like 'Come Down Softly To My Soul' – gospel music revisited by Tav Falco and Panther Burns enthusiasts with a dollop of Can on the side. (Go figure.) I caught them live at a pissy municipal venue in Aylesbury, which I travelled to alone, on the bus from Oxford. The band always used to sit on stools, so the audience followed suit, and squatted on the floor, which left me with a beer-soaked, grimy arse. No doubt it still would have been a memorable experience with the industrial quantities of psychotropic drugs that the band's records seemed designed for, but five pints of stale lager made it quite uncomfortable. The return journey home on the bus was less fun. But that's the sort of thing you did at the time.

As much as I loved these acts, however, they were always going to be confined to the margins. I couldn't see the Spacemen's Sonic Boom ('We're the band that make Joy Division look raunchy,' he once said) or

Gibby Haynes from The Buttholes (who looked like a walking hallucination) ever making *Top of the Pops*. The fact that Gibby was the son of American children's TV presenter 'Mr Peppermint' only made it more improbable. Through new independent distribution companies like Pinnacle, it was easy to hunt their records down in shops, but it wasn't as if there was mass advertising for them. If you wanted to discover acts through the mass media, there was only Peel on the radio and *Snub TV*, a short-lived BBC2 magazine programme, and the *NME* and *Melody Maker*.

By the time I started reading it, the *NME* was devoted to indie acts, but it had hitched its wagon to mincing groups like The Wedding Present and The Smiths, issuing a famous tape called *C86* with a copy of the paper in 1986 (none of your fancy cover-mounted CDs,) featuring such bands. The *Melody Maker* offered more extensive coverage of the groups I liked and was quite happy to stick them on its cover, even if people like J Mascis from Dinosaur Jr stuck out like a sore thumb on the news-stands. I never subscribed to the paper, so holidays meant missing a copy or two and were therefore purgatory. What if I missed a Revolting Cocks album review! One year, I found a current issue on a news-stand in a small town square in Italy, which made the week away for me. (Just pity my parents for tolerating their moping adolescent scouring every other news outlet for seven days prior to that, oblivious to the charms of Tuscany.) And it had some terrific writers – who were able to persuade me to part with my pocket money for records by incredibly obscure bands. The paper ran a cover feature on World Domination Enterprises, a garage rock act with dub tendencies, only good, who had some kind of affiliation to a scary-looking collective of artists called The Mutoid Waste Company. The band made what I consider to be the best album of the era, *Let's Play Domination*, which was also brilliantly packaged in a lurid fluorescent sleeve. No one else I know can remember the record at all and the band have never featured in any rock histories or *Mojo*, yet. (On the other hand, whoever recommended that Band of Susans LP can have it back now.)

In the seventies, of course, the *NME* had been the great champion of punk, running the first live review of The Sex Pistols, at the Screen on the Green in February 1976, by Neil Spencer ('We're not into music . . . We're into chaos,' Rotten told him). An ad for 'two hip young gunslingers' to join the writing team was then placed in the paper, and the young Tony Parsons and Julie Burchill arrived. These were the *NME*'s golden years, when the paper became an integral part of punk culture, as it continues to keep telling its readers.

The *NME* had first been published in 1952, by which time *Melody Maker* had already been chronicling developments in popular music for a quarter of a century. Both titles were aimed at musicians more than fans, and when the *NME* launched its singles chart in November 1952, *Melody Maker* disapproved, complaining that this was a gimmick which focused attention on popularity rather than musical prowess. The *NME* became slightly hipper – in 1958, Elvis swept its annual readers' polls while failing to register at all in *Melody Maker*'s equivalent. It took a long time, however, for both titles to catch up with the spirit of rock and roll. When *Sgt Pepper* was released in 1967, the *NME* simply noted that 'it's a very good LP and will sell like hot cakes'. It took the counter-culture press – titles like *International Times* and *Oz* – to capture the real mood of the times. Jan Wenner's *Rolling Stone*, which began publication in America in '67, treated rock stars like latter-day Caravaggios. This, really, was the point at which rock separated from pop.

Back in the eighties, I still longed to have lived in Swinging London. I still longed for punk. Where was our boat trip down the Thames on Jubilee Day? I was still waiting for the moment. Rock acts always try to hide the fact that they are commercial entities. Rock Svengalis other than Jon Landau – Andrew Loog Oldham, who managed the Stones, Peter Grant, who looked after Led Zeppelin, and McLaren with the Pistols – all waged a kind of phoney war with the industry to preserve the notion of credibility. The bands I liked as a teenager were happy to leave that fight, but paid a price. The focus of most indie acts was internal, self-pitying, miserabilist. (I haven't mentioned The Smiths in any of this. I always hated The Smiths.) Even the heroes of that scene, the Spacemen, MBV, a handful of others, made their own retreat, into sonic texture and getting wasted. At least in that respect there was some connection to the future. Otherwise, indie said it all.

> 'This is black punk rock, and this isn't what people want' – Russell Simmons

Alongside home-grown acts like MBV, at the time I also loved small and gnarly American bands like Dinosaur Jr, who defined the post-baby-boom slacker scene later explored by film-makers such as Richard Linklater and writers like Douglas Coupland. From them, and through reading the *Melody Maker*, I got into a few bands emerging out of the provincial backwater of Seattle. I was a particular fan of Mudhoney, seeing them a couple of times when they toured Britain. I also remember being pleased that the support for that second date was Tad, the 'Fat' Rik Waller of the nascent grunge movement, rather than a group called Nirvana, who had to pull out at the last moment.

I never particularly cared for Nirvana and can remember feeling bemused when they took off. There seemed something contrived about their success, and besides, I wasn't ready to share my scene with morons who only watched MTV. In fact, grunge wasn't America picking up on home-grown bands who had had to go to England first to find some level of critical appreciation (like Jimi Hendrix). It was about America discovering punk fifteen years on. Whatever. It seems that Kurt Cobain felt much the same way as me and – boom – topped himself.

There was another act I really liked when I was at school, Public Enemy, whose radical agenda was explicitly located in the political as well as musical spheres. Driving around north Oxford with my mate after school in his second-hand Mini, I memorised great chunks of the lyrics and became well versed in the appeal of the Honourable Prophet Elijah Mohammad and Louis Farrakhan (who said that all white people were devils). I still maintain that Robert Leslie-Carter, who to this day can rap all the words from 'Fear Of A Black Planet', is a better white MC than Eminem. At least we hadn't gone the whole Ali G hog and were dressed in our shabby school uniforms. But we could never really feel part of what Public Enemy were trying to achieve.

Hip hop was America's authentic punk, but it soon sold its soul too. When Public Enemy had first signed to Def Jam, Russell Simmons, one of the two bosses, complained to his partner Rick Rubin: 'Why? Why do your waste your time with this stuff? No one's ever gonna like this. This is black punk rock, and this isn't what people want.' That proved right. Meanwhile, NWA on the West Coast ('Express Yourself': greatest single ever?) quickly turned the posturing of gangsta rap into a sales slogan. Hip hop today is probably the most corporate form of music in creation. Eminem? Brilliant. But he's also a brilliant fake, peddling an empty threat. Dressing up in your video as Osama Bin Laden? Piss off. But perhaps you can see why Bin Laden's men may have been scared of American pop culture. It is the perfect manifestation of how Western capitalism spreads the poison of Western culture. But let's not perhaps quite go there yet.

> *'The Roses could hardly have been less enthusiastic if we'd suggested a poolside romp with Linda Lusardi'* – NME

In the late eighties something finally happened on English soil which promised to give my own generation its own moment in the sun. The irony was, when acid house finally kicked off, I more or less missed it completely. I never went to Shoom and I never necked six Es in an evening dancing to Danny Rampling. I never failed to find a rave after driving round the M25 for half the night and I've hardly ever understood the real appeal of chill-out albums. That's what being an indie fan had done to me. But I was at the first night of Pure in Edinburgh, another legendary club which played blinding techno, though it was pretty sparsely populated according to my admittedly somewhat warped memories of that evening. And even if I'd wanted to, there was no escaping the chart presence of bands like Inner City and The KLF and 808 State. These last were part of the nascent Madchester scene, and like everyone else I knew I quickly fell in love with the bands that married that classic guitar rock of The Beatles and Byrds with the euphoric groove of acid house: start saying things like 'top' and 'mega' and say hello to The Stone Roses and Happy Mondays! It felt like we were taking over.

'The 1980s were cynical,' said Roses singer Ian Brown at the end of the decade. 'People didn't want to participate. You can wake up one morning and feel negative or positive. Why feel negative? It's better to be positive, to connect.'

The Stone Roses had been around in Manchester since 1985, and were just another indie band. Slowly building their fan base and honing their art, they were revealed to the wider world (south of Watford Gap) in the early summer of 1989. The first inkling I had that something was up was seeing my friend Dan after our A-levels, drinking in the pub, and noticing his flares.

The band had their own look and they talked the talk ('we're the most important group in the world', they said) and walked the walk (trashing the offices of a record company with paint when they fell into dispute). Guitarist John Squire himself painted the bands' record sleeves – the lemon on their dazzling first album was apparently a reference to the *événements* of Paris in 1968, when protesters sucked lemons to counteract the tear gas. They turned their gigs into special events – Blackpool; Ally Pally; Spike Island. It was the complete pop cultural package, even without the funny drugs. Yet buoyed up on a few pills, even white guitar-boys learnt how to dance – even if it wasn't always a pretty sight.

At Spike Island in March 1990, the crowd willed the show into their own Woodstock, even though the Roses were, as so often, rather disappointing live. Among the 30,000 fans who travelled to that gig on a Cheshire nature reserve were two young men known as Bonehead and Guigs, who were so inspired by the show that they went off to find a singer called Liam Gallagher to form their own band. This was the point at which indie apologists finally twigged the allure of old-school rock trappings: the sense of occasion; the studied cool of Ian Brown who had the voice of a lame heifer but the pout and haircut of a real rock idol; the whiff of revolution, of any kind.

Paul Oakenfold deejayed at Spike Island (there wasn't a traditional support act). 'Before the Roses and the Happy Mondays, music was very divided,' he later said. 'You weren't supposed to like dance music and indie music and the Roses were one of the key things that helped break those barriers down by just mixing it all up. If it hadn't been for Spike Island, I wouldn't have been supporting U2 at Wembley Stadium [within] a couple of years.'

Yet John Squire saw it differently. 'I think too much has been made of this indie/dance cross-over,' he said. 'It implies that people think in rigid categories. Are people really so selective in what they listen to? Everyone I know has a cross-section of music in their collection. It's just the love of amplified sound.'

For their 1989 Christmas issue, the *NME* took The Stone Roses to a snowy peak in Switzerland, and tried to get them to recreate the cover of The Beatles' *Help* album, on which the moptops lined up to give a message in semaphore. 'The Roses could hardly have been less enthusiastic if we'd suggested a poolside romp with Linda Lusardi,' the paper reported. That signalled their intent. Here was a band that would never sell out, but aimed to take the game to the enemy's court. 'We should be on *Top of the Pops*,' said Ian Brown. 'I like seeing our record go up and Kylie and Phil Collins go down.' I still have my copy of that paper.

From that mountain top, however, the only way was down, of course. The band got stuck in creative paralysis and started bitching about each other and doing drugs holed up in a recording studio in Wales. And, in fact, they had never been quite the popular sensation we believed: their dazzling debut album peaked in the charts at number 19. (And though Bob Stanley raved about it in the *Melody Maker* – 'this is the one, this is the one . . .' – the *NME* gave it only six out of ten). I saw the Roses only when they finally made their comeback with their disappointing second album, *The Second Coming*, and a UK tour. (Actually, I caught them in Bridlington, on the first night.) But I did see the Happy Mondays in their prime, as well as members of the baggy diaspora like the Inspiral Carpets (roadie: Noel Gallagher), World of Twist and Flowered Up. I bought records by the likes of Paris Angels and Northside. I even tried to find some jeans that were slightly wide in the leg. But frankly by that stage it had all started getting a bit pantomime. The Mondays had two Top 10 hits in 1990 with 'Step On' and 'Kinky Afro' but lost it all on a massive crack binge and started doing things like guest-editing *Penthouse*. Primal Scream had carried the flame too, thanks to Gillespie's encounter with Andy Weatherall and some happy pills, which produced *Screamadelica*, the second bona fide classic of the era after the Roses' debut. But after one all-night session too many, they decided to have a long lie-in, and came back as a lunchtime pub guitar band.

As for acid house and the emergent dance and ecstasy culture, it wasn't long before the government put through legislation banning big outdoor raves. It was difficult to mount any kind of opposition, particularly because that drug hardly encourages hand-to-hand engagement with the world. As Jarvis Cocker said, half the E-heads left half their brains somewhere in a field in Hampshire.

The scene also started to mutate at a bewildering pace. People like James Palumbo, whose father was a former head of the Arts Council, turned clubbing into just another leisure experience with his Ministry brand, leaving true adherents scrambling to devise new strains of music, with their own mini-sub-cultures, to keep ahead of the game:' appy 'ardkore and gabba, drum and bass and two step, deep house and nu progressive . . . and so on. I couldn't keep up. If the major labels didn't decide to bleed all the life out a scene, it was because its adherents were too small in numbers to make it worth their while.

Depressing news. The year which saw The Stone Roses' giddying rise also witnessed Stock, Aitken and Waterman's most successful twelve months yet. The trio won the Ivor Novello Songwriter of the Year award for the third consecutive year and were the number-one independent publishing company in Britain. In fact, they were the number-two corporate publishing company as well, second only to EMI, which only beat them by 2 per cent. And EMI had 16,000 writers and bought songs in from all over the place; SAW had just the three of them and they did it all themselves.

But Kylie had declared she wanted to be the new Madonna, despite the fact that she was outselling her by three to one, and said she wanted to start dressing like a prostitute in her videos. And Jason Donovan, meanwhile, had announced he was a Happy Mondays fan. Perhaps there was hope yet.

> *'Look, I'm a product of my generation. I'm delighted at the success of British pop music'* – Tony Blair

By the time The Stone Roses emerged blinking into the sun from hibernation in 1995, Oasis were looming large. I saw them at the cramped Astoria in London before the release of their first album, *Definitely Maybe*, in September 1994, and couldn't quite see what the fuss was about. By the time of their homecoming gig at Maine Road in Manchester in 1996 and the vast

Knebworth shows later that same year, they were simply in their element. The best pub rock band on the planet.

Zoë and I watched at Maine Road from the directors' box, among the PR hordes and other journalists and friends of the band, drinking from the big free bar. But we sneaked down to the pitch right in front of the stage for the end. It may have been the best gig of my life. At Knebworth (the first of two nights) we watched from halfway into the crowd of 80,000. Even from there, Liam looked fantastic, mouthy and cool, despite his white cricket jumper. It didn't matter if we couldn't hear him, because everyone in the crowd sang along to pretty much every song. Here was that sense of communion again. And this was the era when my lot took control, the era of Britpop.

There was something deliriously exciting about Oasis' famous spat with Blur, which came to a head when the two groups released singles on the same day in the summer of 1995. Bong! Bong! Bong! And there it was on *News at Ten* too. When Jarvis Cocker invaded the stage during Michael Jackson's ludicrous performance at the Brits in February 1996 and wiggled his skinny tush in front of the world, it seemed like the oceans would part and mountains crumble.

There was some of the energy of the acid house scene left in there too, most evident in the arrival of a group like The Chemical Brothers, who hung out with the new rock aristocracy at their regular deejaying haunt, the Heavenly Social.

Some of my friends who had been at university in Manchester knew Tom and Ed Chemical, and the Social took place round the corner from where I used to live north of Oxford Street in London on Sunday nights. We were there from the start, nodding hello to Noel and Bobby Gillespie from Primal Scream as if we knew them well – as if we knew them at all – and going upstairs for a pint when Tricky came on the decks, playing an unlistenable-to mix of eclectic nonsense.

There was also a nice moment a couple of years later when Oasis staged a series of gigs at Earls Court. I was backstage with Zoë for a pre-show drink at one, and had to borrow twenty quid off Tom Chemical when I realised to my horror that this time the bar wasn't gratis. Suddenly Kate Moss joined the circle, and here we were at the epicentre of the New Swinging London. That's my answer to the 'What did you do in the Britpop wars, Daddy?' question from the children. It was quite easy to play it cool – a few mumbled grunts sufficed, rather than Wildean witticisms. Still. *Fucking hell*.

Newsweek called London 'the coolest city on the planet' in 1996, an observation quoted by John Major in a speech as Prime Minister at the Lord Mayor's Banquet at Guildhall that November. The March 1997 issue of *Vanity Fair* magazine carried a picture of Liam and his then wife Patsy Kensit on its cover, with the slogan 'London Swings Again'. Inside, over the course of twenty-four pages, journalist David Kamp took the pulse of the capital, kicking off his piece with some chronological inexactitude with an explicit parody of Colin MacInnes' 1957 novel *Absolute Beginners*: 'Move it along, Granddad, you're getting in the way of The Scene! . . . Dear Old Blighty pulses anew with the good vibrations of an epic-scale youthquake!'

Kamp perspicaciously lumped Britpop in with the rise of the new Britart and the success of British couturiers such as Alexander McQueen and the arrival of restaurants such as Terence Conran's Quaglino's. Conran was old enough to remember Swinging London Mark I (that title bestowed by a piece in *Time* magazine in April 1966 . . . 'This spring as never before, London is switched on'). 'What you must understand,' Conran told *Vanity Fair*, 'is that Swinging London was an absolute *microcosm* compared to what is going on now . . . There's a much greater distribution of wealth among young people.'

The magazine also interviewed the Leader of the Opposition, Tony Blair, who was asked whether a rock star would be welcome at Number 10 if Labour won the imminent general election. 'Well, I think we'll wait until we get there before deciding that!' said the man who had played in a rock band called Ugly Rumours at Oxford. 'But look, I'm a product of my generation. I'm delighted at the success of British pop music.'

Yet there was something rotten at the heart of this fantasy. For one thing, for all their mouthy posturing, the Britpop bands were always playing the game for the sake of a key industry earner and precious little more. It was hard to see what the point of this revolution was. Oasis were signed to Creation, which had started life as an independent but were really fully fledged major-label rock giants. 'Fifteen years ago, Noel Gallagher wouldn't have wanted to have been seen dead in the singles chart,' Pete Waterman said to me. 'And any progressive rock artiste fifteen years would have spat on the record companies' grave if they said go on *Top of the Pops*.' Instead, Oasis bought into mainstream values, and the mainstream took over.

Closet conservatives, the band also made a virtue of their heritage. When *Mojo* wanted to photograph the group for the front cover of their 1994 Christmas issue posing on top of Primrose Hill in exactly the spot where Gered Mankowitz had shot the Stones for the cover of *Between The Buttons* in January 1966 . . . they happily complied.

There was nothing political about Britpop either – or if there was the politics were very Little England. There were interesting collaborations – like a Chemical Brothers track featuring Noel Gallagher – but for the most part the emphasis was on writing quality tunes using proper old guitars and none of your modern fancy stuff, thank you very much. By the time of the Oasis vs Blur singles showdown, both bands were in end-of-pier territory, too. Blur made the video for their single, 'Country House', with Damien Hirst, which carried echoes of The Beatles hiring Peter Blake to make the sleeve for *Sgt Pepper*. But there was nothing very clever about it, just a bunch of Benny Hill birds getting their tits out. Oasis were only more honestly part of the new lad culture. Perhaps this was our Woodstock, but the right to walk into a newsagent's and buy a copy of *Loaded* magazine without any shame didn't seem like the greatest of victories. If Oasis extended the parameters of their social ambitions, it was only to start hanging out at the Met Bar and date celebrities. (Which was a bit more *FHM* or *Heat*, if you're thinking periodicals.) They were harbingers of the new celebrity culture. For the kind of bands I'd always liked, the game was finally up.

> *'Fookin' hell! They remind me of the fookin' Monkees!'*
> *– Liam Gallagher*

What happened? 'Whatever happened to my rock and roll?' sang a group called Black Rebel Motorcycle Club in the early months of 2002. Along with a handful of other acts – The Hives, The Strokes, The Soundtrack of Our Lives – they were hailed as saviours of a moribund rock scene. That seemed like a bunch of arse to me.

For one thing, BRMC took their name from Marlon Brando's gang of bikers in the fifties movie *The Wild One*, which was a crushing cliché. For another, the irony in the lyrics of that song just didn't work either. If the band didn't know the answer to their own question, then what the bloody hell were they doing there? They kicked up an agreeable racket all right, but there was no real stink of brimstone about them either. It's easy to act the tit about things like this, and part of the problem was probably that I was too old for this type of music by then. Perhaps it's hard to get worked up about a band if you're listening to them on the crappy CD-player at seven in the morning, trying to spoon-feed a toddler. Yet you wanted these bands to provide some sort of opposition to the manufactured pop acts that were clogging up the charts. How dismaying that, in their own way, they seemed no less artificial. Of course, there were differences – in the haircuts and suchlike (at least you didn't have to worry about your perma-tan if you were in a rock band) – but really, these were superficial.

Launching the hype for Oasis' *Heathen Chemistry* album, Liam Gallagher made a characteristically pertinent observation. 'I don't see The Strokes as dangerous, or The Hives,' he said. 'Fookin' hell! They remind me of the fookin' Monkees!' But of course he couldn't exclude his own group from that criticism.

Record companies knew from Oasis that bands like these were eminently marketable. If you defined rock narrowly – young white lads playing guitars and never mind the business about dope, guns and fucking in the street (to use the early MC5's phrase) – rock was a reliable brand. 'People talk about commercialism as a dirty word,' according to Pete Waterman in his autobiography. 'That's bullshit. Travis are one of the finest commercial pop bands around, but because it's disguised within the rock genre it's respected.'

'Writing a Noel Gallagher song is easy because his fans are buying an ethos, whereas kids buy Westlife or

Steps because they like them,' is what he said to me. 'I have to visit the coalface every day to find another nugget and no one's going to give me a million pounds if I don't.'

According to this view, it's rock which is peddling a lie, not pop – the lie of its own image. In March 2002 it was reported that Travis had been kept awake the night before a gig by noisy members of S Club 7 staying in the same hotel. At four in the morning singer Fran Healy finally put his foot down. 'I couldn't believe the noise coming from next door. I finally banged on their door,' he recalled. 'I said, "If you don't mind, some of us are trying to sleep because we've got a show to play tomorrow night."' All the same, I bet the Travis boys woke up to find their sheets damp – and that's why they're called bed-wetters.

By this time, there were very few dissimilarities between rock and pop. In pop's favour, in fact, was that pop stars were generally more glamorous and bitchy than their rock cohorts. Actually, at times, the pop scene looked quite fun to me, for the first time since 1981. And who kicked that off? Before S Club 7 there were The Spice Girls, queens of the new Swinging London – at least, *Vanity Fair* pictured them as such. *The Face* put them on their cover in that same month in 1997. Posh declared: 'We want to be a household name. We want to be a Fairy Liquid or an Ajax.'

In the piece, interviewer Chris Heath told Posh that her sort of twisted London-y, slightly-hoity-toity-but-not drawl made her sound like Justine from Elastica. 'She's got hairier armpits,' Posh replied, which seemed to sum it all up.

4

BIG BROTHER AND HOW TV WENT POP

> *'I love opera and classical music. My hobbies are cricket, food and restoring old steam engines. And what do they call me? Vulgar'* – Peter Bazalgette

Big Brother, the brainchild of Dutch TV executive John de Mol, was first broadcast in Holland in the autumn of 1999. By the final episode of the series, when the winner was declared, it had the second-highest ratings of any programme that year. The highest? A news programme covering the declaration of war in Kosovo. 'What war in Kosovo?' I wondered for at least a second when I first read that.

Watching the three series of *Big Brother* in this country, I often wondered whether it was making me more stupid. I tried to switch off my TV set and go and do something less boring instead – but felt powerless in its grip.

When *Big Brother* first aired in Britain in the summer of 2000, pop music was in the doldrums. Since Britpop, there hadn't been a pop phenomenon that had seized the public mood. Perhaps the problem lay in pop music itself: there was a chilling inevitability about the success of prefabricated teeny acts, while the rock bands to whom you'd normally turn for a bit of reaction were themselves utterly ineffectual. It seemed that *Big Brother* marked something new. The characters had entered the house as normal people but emerged to crowds of screaming fans. Idiots like Craig, the Scouser who won the first series, were turned into fully fledged celebrities, fixtures of the tabloids and *Heat* magazine. There was also substantial coverage in the broadsheets, largely weighted towards ponderous analysis. The energy of pop culture was now to be found in a TV show.

Of course there were other great TV events before *Big Brother*. The Coronation in 1953 caused sales of television sets to sky-rocket, while the big question of my pre-pop childhood was 'Who shot JR?'. But whereas previous shows that had drawn record-breaking audiences were reports of state occasions or sporting fixtures (or pop concerts to feed the world), or involved dramatic narratives that Aeschylus would have understood, *Big Brother* fell between these two stools. Rather, it created a quasi-real world in which events and people's lives were transformed into meta-narratives. In other words, quite often it was difficult to know what the bollocks it was.

Just as Hollywood and the music industry have fallen in love with the High Concept, television today is all about finding the killer format. John de Mol's company Endemol is devoted to dreaming up new concepts that can be adapted for different marketplaces. In *The People's Game*, for example, viewers manage a football team, making decisions through interactive multiple-choice questions. There should be a strong human interest because a docu-soap narrative follows the lives of the girlfriends and wives of the players too. Selling the idea, Endemol promised that the show was carefully designed so that it could be adapted to different national sports, such as baseball, ice hockey or rugby, boasting that this 'may just be the way that all sport will be covered in the future'. Sounds kind of neat, no?

Big Brother was based on a format of almost mathematical beauty, yielding results of astonishing complexity from a very simple premise. John de Mol considered just two rules sacred to every territory. One: contestants can have no place to escape the cameras. Two: contestants must have no contact with events in the outside world. The only time this was broken was in America on 11 September, when contestants were told about the terrorist strikes because one of them had family in New York. *Big Brother* was running in seven other countries at the time, and the news was kept secret in all of them. Otherwise TV bosses were allowed to mess with the blueprint as much as they liked. In Argentina there was a guest appearance from Diego Maradona, to the delight of the housemates, while in Norway the contestants were similarly thrilled to have Status Quo perform for them. (Which probably tells you all you need to know about the difference between Latin and Scandinavian countries.)

Eighteen countries picked up on the Dutch format

within the space of two years, and only in America was it not a big hit. Sex was the great question everywhere, but the format threw up interesting different national attitudes. In Britain the talking point in the second series of the show was the blossoming romance between Helen and Paul. In Anglo-Saxon fashion, they refused to cop off with each other lest the cameras catch them at it. In Norway, one couple copulated six times in one day, the *Big Brother* record. The programme never broke viewing figures in this country – though it sometimes seemed that way given the amount of media coverage – but the size of the global audience for the format was staggering.

In some ways I wasn't the perfect *Big Brother* viewer. The programme was picked up for British screens by independent production company Bazal. According to the official *Big Brother* book: 'Bazal was a natural home for an innovative and experimental series, having pioneered shows like *Changing Rooms*, *Ground Force* and *Ready, Steady, Cook*, all of which have an element of unpredictability and participation by ordinary viewers.'

I've watched all those programmes. Even I'm not sure I concur with Peter Bazalgette, the boss of Bazal, who claims that 'now is the true golden age' of TV. He has argued, however, that naysayers complaining that his shows dumb television down are the 'lazy, old, unthinking, miserable brigade'.

'There are people in TV, many of whom are in their fifties,' he continued, 'who think the world is getting worse. They've created a cultural depression, constantly harping on about how television is no good . . . You never hear people in their twenties and thirties speaking that way. Like them, I feel good about the future.' The sort of critics he had in mind were people like media commentator Stephen Glover, who singled Bazalgette out as a force of social evil in a piece for the *Daily Mail* at the time of the third series of *Big Brother*. 'There has always been rubbish on television but at least it used to be fairly harmless,' Glover wrote. 'Twenty, 30, 40 years ago there were many producers, often idealistic and Left-wing, who wanted to make programmes which enriched the human condition. Of course, there are still such people about, but they are in retreat.' Well, good to hear a word for the Trots in that paper.

Yet I'm in my early thirties and can't remember programmes like Kenneth Clark's *Civilisation*, the example of serious programming from the past that is always held up to shame us. All the same, we did grow up with *The Late Review* and other supposedly highbrow chat shows. When the *NME* interviewed The Stone Roses for that Christmas issue, the journalist got into a row with the band about the nature of pop, following several hours drinking brandy. The following morning the great bassist Mani reflected, 'Well, it certainly did turn into *After Dark* last night, didn't it?' And today there are channels dedicated to the arts, like Artsworld and BBC4.'

But I don't really use the telly to learn about the

things these stations waffle on about. Rather, my complaint is based on the aimless junk – those Top 10 programmes and the stuff described by that *Sun* TV editor – not being entertaining enough. There are precious few shows that I would make an appointment to watch.

When I was a kid I would scurry home from school and make myself my tea and a bed on the sofa in the room in which we had the telly (so middle class that it wasn't the sitting room) and forbid entry to other members of the family. That would be the weekly screening of *Monkey* – the surreal adventures of a bloke with mutton-chop sideburns pretending to be a superhero monkey, plus Pigsy, Sandy and Tripitaka, dubbed incredibly badly from Japanese into English, and some spectacularly cack-handed special effects. Mind you, it was based on the sixteenth-century Chinese epic *Hsi Yu Chi*, so perhaps I did learn something from it.

There were also programmes I always watched with my sister, such as *Dallas* and later the early *EastEnders* and maybe occasionally *Neighbours*. The Ramsay Street soap aired in Australia in 1985, starting on British screens on 27 October 1986. Initially it was only broadcast in the mornings and at lunch-time, but when the daughter of the BBC's then head of programming, Michael Grade, told him that she and her friends had grown obsessed with the show during the holidays, he scheduled it in a post-school time slot as well. It quickly became its own phenomenon – attracting audiences of up to 16 million. By the time I was at university, I'd grown into the habit of looking for a

TV every lunch-time to check on what was happening in the street.

On the music side there was *Top of the Pops* on Thursday evenings, and from when I was eleven, in 1982, *The Tube* on Channel 4 on Friday nights. I just about remember the *Top of the Pops* dancers, though the girls I viewed in a state of pre-sexual boredom must have been Legs and Co. and finally Zoo rather than the fabled Pan's People. Then came videos – the dancers were retired in 1983 – so half my formative pop memories involve video images. *The Tube* – and then *The Word*, I guess – provided a happy antidote because they featured only live bands, but at the cost of spazzy presenting. The only other music programme that sticks in my mind is that *Snub TV*. It was limping on when The Stone Roses came around. I remember an item where it showed them in the studio mixing 'Fool's Gold' months before it came out and wondering where I could get myself an orange T-shirt like Ian Brown's (perhaps his came from Affleck's Palace, that fabled nexus of baggy fashion, but I didn't think there was anywhere like that in Oxford).

Today, I usually get back from work too late to see *Top of the Pops*, and if we are going out it tends to be on a Friday evening. I quite like *Later . . .*, and the producer's tastes match mine pretty closely, and I enjoy a nostalgic fondness for Jools Holland from his days on *The Tube*. But sparks rarely fly between the different bands on the show, and it's not very interesting visually. There's no *TV* in the show, only music. And it's on a bit late for me to be arsed to stay up for it.

Mostly I just sit in lassitude in front of nonsense like *Changing Rooms*, waiting for ten o'clock and *Big Brother* to start. That doesn't make me a moron, necessarily. I can empathise with Peter Bazalgette, who complained of his critics: 'I love opera and classical music. My hobbies are cricket, food and restoring old steam engines. And what do they call me? Vulgar.'

For all its own vulgarity, *Big Brother* was actually an incredibly sophisticated piece of work that treated its audience like grown-ups. In this country this was reflected in the very look of the show, which despite appearances was apparently smarter than in Holland. The sets looked a bit wonky and cameras occasionally came into shot. But according to executive producer Ruth Wrigley: 'The audience we attracted understand television, they've grown up with it, they know its grammar. The crew was used to working in light entertainment and they assumed we'd have the sort of set where a presenter like Cilla Black would walk on and everything would happen smoothly and seamlessly around her. But that's not what I wanted. I wanted it to look live and exciting, I wanted viewers – and the contestants who were evicted – to see the control room, to get an idea of all the behind-the-scenes work.' In other words, modern viewers were no mugs. *Big Brother*, of course, shared some of its genetic material with docu-soaps like the BBC's highly successful *Airport* and *Driving School*, which purported to show real people doing real things. There was also an affinity with a new breed of shows like *Who Wants to Be a Millionaire?* and *The Weakest Link*, which could be corralled into the category of cruelty TV because of the way in which they played remorselessly on their contestants' insecurities ('Are you sure?'). The formats for these two programmes sold globally.

Popstars brought these two sub-genres together. The show was distinguished by the discrepancy between the contestants' perception of their abilities and reality, which proved so visibly – and audibly – entertaining.

At the bottom end of the reality scale was something like *Touch the Truck*, an endurance game show. The twenty contestants had to spend a week touching a truck. That was it. They were allowed ten-minute toilet breaks every two hours and fifteen-minute food breaks every six hours. One sleep-deprived competitor let go of the vehicle after he imagined he had seen a pile of chocolates next to him. Another thought he had turned into an ocean liner. The show was broadcast daily on Channel 5 and broadcast twenty-four hours a day on the channel's website. The winner was the last person left touching the vehicle after six days. He won the truck.

Some commentators sought to locate our fascination with this species of junk in a socio-political context. In an article for the *Observer* that is framed and hung in the offices of Henry's House – the PR company that looked after the first two series of *Big Brother* and *Pop Idol* – Germaine Greer wrote that watching *Big*

Brother 2 was 'about as dignified as looking through the keyhole in your teenage child's bedroom door. To do it occasionally would be shameful; to get hooked on it is downright depraved.' She mentioned that 'Pope John Paul II has denounced reality TV as incompatible with human dignity'. Wow.

The celebrated academic went on to argue that we are fascinated with *Big Brother* and other reality shows because they tap into our contemporary experience of surveillance cameras and government interference in our lives. Other pundits in the right-wing press said it was all to do with the idea of the EU. Greer perceptively noted that artists were similarly preoccupied with such subject matters. Mona Hatoum, for instance, has made video pieces in which she has put tiny cameras and fibre-optic cables inside her body so we can see her sphincter working. Funnier if it had been the bodies of those other journalists.

Perhaps Greer at least was on to something. Watching the first series of *Big Brother*, the *Daily Telegraph*'s art critic, Richard Dorment, realised what Tracey Emin was trying to communicate in her work. Pieces like the tent on which the queen of Britart embroidered the names of everyone she'd ever shagged could be read as deft prefigurations of the public's new-found prurient interest in the lives of others.

There's a wider point. In half the tabloids and other broadsheets, the new Britart was rubbished as a lot of incomprehensible garbage. But much of it was surprisingly old fashioned, in fact. The materials might be novel – unkempt beds, dead sharks and so on – but there was a narrative point to this work. Emin and Hirst et al. were storytellers, much in the manner of classical artists of the past, except here the focus tended towards the intensely personal.

Given all this, I like to think that *Big Brother* is a work of art in itself – a bit like one of Andy Warhol's films, only with less attractive models. Someone should enter it for the Turner Prize.

But perhaps that kind of thinking is the product of watching *Big Brother* live late into the night. If people all over the world are fascinated by the sex lives of strangers, doesn't that suggest an equally primal urge? The need to gossip about them. As Desmond Morris, the *Naked Ape* guy, said: '*Big Brother* appeals to the nosy-parker in us, peering over the garden fence and then gossiping about what we see . . . We all spy on the same neighbours and share the same knowledge about them.' That seems like a pretty straightforward and convincing explanation for the show's success, particularly if you are of the opinion that, ever since the start of mass industrialisation in the nineteenth century, man has become estranged from fellow man. In other words, people don't know their neighbours any more but *Big Brother* affords us an imagined community – a surrogate version of real life. Sure enough, watching the first three series of the show, I felt as if the contestants were even part of the family (even Jade).

Some commentators criticised the show because the contestants were so thick and unappealing. I guess that's their prerogative – in fact sometimes I shared their view. I sort of hated Craig from the first series. His stated ambitions before entering the house were: 'To be well-liked and popular, and to become a singer/performer.' His favourite band was Oasis. He said the only book he had ever read was Sylvester Stallone's autobiography. Among the things he packed to bring with him were two magazines (*Men's Health* and *FHM*), two bottles of white wine, five condoms and a set of earplugs. He seemed to represent that conformist endpoint of Britpop culture. And Jade, meanwhile, was no 'Mr Heinstein'.

There were also repellent contestants like Nasty Nick, but at least he afforded us the 'unique opportunity ... to see the manipulative personality in action', in the words of ubiquitous pop psychologist Dr Raj Persaud, who located this archetype in Machiavelli's Prince. Part of the delight of the first two series, however, was that the people left towards the end of the show were mostly so likeable. The fact that others clearly shared my fondness for them – and that Brian, winner of the second series, was not persecuted for being gay (more remarkably, that lesbian Anna secured the runner's-up spot on the first) – made it all the more refreshing. The vision of Britain that *Big Brother* presented was multiracial and more tolerant than a hippy commune in upstate California circa 1967. And even Craig and the gormless Kate Lawler were more or less harmless.

I found myself wanting to agree with Lord Bragg of Wigton – aka Melvyn Bragg – for the first time in my life, when he argued that the best of contemporary television is popular because normal people are finally able to see themselves portrayed on screen: 'On television they have, for the first time in the history of our culture, taken over the world. We see ourselves . . . in *Popstars* and *Big Brother*, we see ourselves in *The Royle Family*, watching them watching . . .'

What of those snobs? Hadn't they ever seen something like a Ken Loach film and recognised that there's beauty inside everyone? Paul ('I've lived my life like an international rock star') calculated that in the space of the six weeks he spent in the house with Helen ('I love blinking I do') in *Big Brother*'s second series, they had enjoyed a year and a half's conversation, which was actually a smart way of saying that they talked utter waffly bollocks to each other. But I found a certain poetry in the banality of their exchanges – and it was such a great love story. Who wasn't moved when Paul told the other housemates, 'I do fancy Helen, and it's purely weird, 'cos I fancy Helen's personality,' and she looked flushed and said, 'It's like all these lights like whizzing past . . . It's like "Woooh"!'

The initial producer of *Big Brother* on Channel 4 was Conrad Green, who went on to boss *Popstars* on ITV. According to Green, the success of both series was straightforward. 'I think all good TV entertainment shows are about people ultimately,' he said. 'What makes a really good entertainment show is ways of bringing the drama of real life into a controlled environment. So quizzes like *Millionaire* are fantastic because they bring real human dilemmas into a format. Shows such as *Friends Like These* and *Weakest Link* are successful in drawing stuff out of ordinary people. Similarly, Barrymore is brilliant as a figurehead but what he's absolutely excellent at is realising the comedy in real people. I don't think there's that much difference between that and *Popstars* and *Big Brother*.' Fair enough. Yet *Big Brother* played with just that controlled environment in a radical fashion. It was pretty far out to be able to watch the live feed of the household in the early hours on Channel 4 or latterly on the station's new spin-off E4. When the channel was launched in 2001 it provided viewers with the opportunity to watch twenty hours of *BB* footage a day – and to the surprise of executives, this coverage proved to be the biggest hit of their first year, rather than expensively acquired first runs of *Friends* and *ER*.

But *Big Brother* never told the whole truth.

I was a fan of the show, but only to the extent that I watched the edited highlights every night throughout the course of all three series. The climax of each week was always Friday, eviction night, when someone made the walk of shame from the house, with Davina.

The unique point about *Big Brother* was that we had a say in who went, voting by phone or computer or mobile gadget, or finally through our digital tellies, against one of two or more contestants nominated by the household each week. The programme was interactive.

The fact that someone left the house each week

changed the dynamic of the environment, so the contestants left would have a new social situation to organise. It increased the gossip factor also. But voting for who should leave made us feel as if we were participating in events too – in the lives of the contestants. Soap operas work because we feel as if we know the characters involved; *Big Brother* made us part of the dialogue with them. The TV screen had been breached.

In fact, *Big Brother* was built around a unique balance of power. The producers could shape the show, but only to a certain extent; the participants could shape their destiny, but only to a certain extent; and the audience could direct the show, but only to a certain extent. Amazingly, there was no one in charge of this cock-eyed shooting-match. 'There's this strange triangle of control,' Conrad Green admitted, 'which makes everyone feel like they participate in it much more.' In other words, as John de Mol said, *Big Brother* is 'one of the most democratic projects in the world'.

Big Brother was often billed as a social experiment because we got to see a group of strangers interacting with each other in a strange house for weeks on end and in detail quite unparalleled. But it was much more than that – much more than something like BBC1's earnest *Castaway*, in which a bunch of pseudo-hippies got it together on a Scottish island for half a year. *Big Brother* was an experiment in the nature of modern culture. And because that balance of power between the participants was so open-ended, it made the format open to abuse. That made it all the more fascinating.

Big Brother really did look like the ultimate reality show, but it's very hard to say that anything you saw could be called an accurate representation of real life. In fact, reality TV was always a troublesome concept. After *Popstars*, Conrad Green was lured to the BBC to head a new 'factual entertainment' department. That sounds like posh for what we're talking about, but he disputed the usefulness of the term, calling it 'a rather lazy moniker'.

Big Brother was meant to show life in the house as it really was, but the fact that the viewers couldn't watch every camera angle at once, the fact that it was edited, and edited to highlights for the viewer's consumption, meant it was a lie. For the highlights show, the editors skilfully strung events together in ways that seemed to emphasise certain storylines and exaggerated the traits of certain personalities. As Vanessa Feltz observed of her appearance on the celebrity version in 2001 – with accuracy: 'I was edited to look like Jack Nicholson in *The Shining*.' (Then again . . .)

In a bid to boost ratings, the programme-makers could also tamper with the physical elements of the show – dividing the house in two with steel bars in the third series – in the hope of generating some drama. They could also choose what type of person they wanted in the house, and progressively went with a telegenic demographic. Certainly, by the time of the third series, the producers were picking people in their early twenties who were likely to fuck or fight. The programme became more and more like a game show. Audience share for the third series was up by over 50 per cent on the first throughout even the comparable early weeks. (Channel 4 wasn't supposed to be interested in viewing figures, but over the course of its twenty-year history – it was founded in November 1982 – that utopian notion seemed to have been quietly forgotten.)

So the contestants were at the mercy of *Big Brother*, and *Big Brother* grew increasingly less benign. At the same time, it became clear right from the first series that while contestants would sign up for *Big Brother* as ordinary joes, they would emerge from the house as temporary fixtures of the popular media. The experience could be terrifying. As Josh, the one who looked so cool in the second series, observed, reality TV shows 'suck you up and spit you out'. It was left to the programme-makers to put safety barriers in place, and sure enough they made potential candidates visit psychologists, while a comprehensive after-show care package was put in place.

Good thing too. Eighty-five per cent of the public voted against Stuart, the boring one, at the end of the first week of the first series. He was booed like a pantomime villain leaving of the house. The first person to be pushed on the third series, Lynne – though another contestant had already jumped of her own accord (in fact, they could leave of their own volition) – was hissed and jeered without that irony. On the other hand, however, Lynne was still invited on to Graham Norton's TV chat show after the event and treated like a figure of national interest, while Jade turned herself into some kind of superstar after her appearance. As indeed had 'Nasty' Nick and nice Brian, and some of the earlier contestants. Even Craig found himself a job on cable telly, presenting a DIY show.

In Poland, meanwhile, a contestant from their version of *Big Brother* was elected to parliament following his appearance on the show, and in Denmark another guy went on to make an album that went to number one in his country for twenty-five weeks.

In other words, when people entered the *Big Brother* household, they entered a Faustian pact; their prize was a measure of contemporary fame. This meant that the number of people applying to be on the programme over the course of the first three series soared – from 20,000 hopefuls first time round to 150,000 for the third. It also ensured that no one entered the house with an open mind about the nature of the experiment. The *Big Brother* household was increasingly filled with exhibitionists. Exposure became the point of taking part, not the price. The contestants were narcissists, who insisted on sharing their feelings with each other as if this were a communal therapy session or *Oprah* or *Trisha*. Anyone who didn't want to be part of all the group hugs – or more – was made to feel weird. It was sick! And it was all the more sick because it spoke with some truthfulness of the aspirations of a generation, which was mine.

Of course, I've fantasised about what life would be like in there with them – just as I've dreamt of winning the Lottery – but the reality would clearly be terrible. I'd welcome the extra sleep and the lack of childcare duties or responsibilities of any kind. Bliss! But I'd also go stir-crazy. And I'm certain that my well-being wouldn't be helped by the other contestants. There is something very odd about wanting to share every waking moment of your life with eleven strangers, let alone every waking and sleeping moment with millions of viewers through the scrutiny of twenty-six cameras and thirty microphones. The people who enter the house are not a cross-section of society and nor are they sane. But it's a very modern madness.

Even I was often bored – though not disgusted – by the contestants' endless fart and willy jokes and puerile antics in the third series. I actually found myself agreeing with the *Daily Mail* that these might be 'the 12 most awful people in Britain', though that did seem a bit much coming from a bunch of venal hypocrites who declared that henceforth the paper would be a '*Big Brother* Free Zone', but two days later gave up most of page nine to report that Sunita had left. (The *Mail* claimed that now she was out of the house, she was a '*Big Brother* Free Zone' herself and therefore legitimate copy fodder. Ha!) And yet I was still watching too.

What of the viewers' responsibilities? There was something barbaric – a touch of bread and circuses – about the frenzy of the crowds outside the house on eviction night each week. But was it really for real – or were the teenagers with the 'Fuck me Spencer' banners really parodying a ritual, a ritual most recently founded in pop culture? Did the contestants really mind the jeers? And was what we'd been watching of the people in the house really real itself?

A large part of *Big Brother*'s appeal, for me, was that the show operated on all these different levels. Was it 'only a game show', as the contestants on the second series kept singing, or were we watching a mirror of real life? There was a mediated fantasy going on there.

In all, it was a bit of a head-fuck, but perhaps this is just the reaction of an old rocker. I really loved the idea that the format could go off the rails at any moment. The problem was built into the format of the premise, which in itself was kind of rock and roll. There was a streak of that nihilism there which has also informed rock from Robert Johnson through to Kurt Cobain and those gimps from Slipknot, I suppose.

I'm guessing that the people who went down to the studio set each Friday night were more Westlife fans.

In fact, I never entered into a dialogue with the *Big Brother* contestants beyond tuning in to watch. I never voted. Neither was I interested in all the add-on features. In its own publicity, Endemol boasted that: 'The show has created a stream of communication driven by real-life content and is sustained by the audiences who are offered the options of the internet, traditional and mobile telephone, and interactive TV. But it is more than a matter of just offering several media platforms with dedicated content. Combining media and driving traffic between the platforms increasingly strengthens the hype and creates an unprecedented "stickiness" and brand awareness.' (Stickiness is a great buzz word of the Internet; it's all to do with how you keep customers involved in your website once they've entered it.)

'If one thing has been proven,' the Endemol manifesto continued, 'it's the eagerness of modern consumers to be involved in as many ways as possible. Spearheaded by massive TV coverage, the community has found its way to interactive media, with cross media links to all platforms. TV, website, email, SMS, WAP, and interactive TV refer to each other and keep the fans updated. More importantly, these media keep the community involved by means of voting, chatting, playing and other options.' In other words, the format provided fearsome ways of pulling you into *Big Brother*.

I'm not interested in SMS or WAP or whatever, but lots of young consumers are, and the money made from these services also profited the programme-makers. If *Big Brother*, with its screaming teenage fans and saturation media coverage, looked like a piece of contemporary pop culture, it could also teach the practitioners of that culture some lessons.

As it was, I thought I might have been bored by the second series already, but in fact it was fascinating to try to figure out which of the new contestants were acting self-consciously, and now that we knew what had happened to 'Nasty' Nick et al it was interesting to guess what their motives might have been in entering the show. In the third, the gimmicks kept things ticking over.

5

CELEBRITY CULTURE AND *HEAT*

> *'There's a strong part of me that's a twenty-five-year-old showbusiness fan from Norwich called Julie'* – Mark Frith

After the terrible events of 11 September 2001, Piers Morgan, the editor of the *Daily Mirror*, declared that the day 'may well have redefined tabloid newspapers in as dramatic a way as it will redefine American foreign policy'. From now on, Morgan seemed to promise, there would be less celebrity fluff in his paper, more hard news reporting. The following spring he relaunched the paper, changing the colour of the masthead from red to black in order to distinguish it from the *Sun* and the *Daily Star*. It emerged then that the road to his personal Damascus had involved my favourite reality TV show.

'I remember sitting in my office one night watching this garbage and thinking: has it really come to this?' he reflected. 'For the first time in thirty years, people in this country are rejecting the *Big Brother*-style trivia they so adored . . . and are realising there are more important things in the world.'

But it wasn't quite that straightforward. On 12 September, there had been no 3am, the *Mirror*'s celebrity gossip column. But on 13 September the world returned to normal, with the page back in its rightful place, bringing us news of an *EastEnders* actress dancing on a table and 'It Girl' Lady Victoria Hervey's most recent shopping spree. At the relaunch a few months later Morgan took the opportunity to double the column's space. He met his critics halfway, and conceded that the paper was about 'serious news and serious gossip'.

Nonetheless: 'September 11 concentrated my mind and made me realise that you can afford to be quite bold with celebrities, you don't have to suck up to them any more . . . 11 September empowered us to put celebrities back in their box.'

He wasn't alone in feeling this way. In America, the grand doyenne of the magazine world, *Vanity Fair*, ran a pompous editorial calling for less celebrity tittle-tattle and more journalistic gravitas after the terrorist attacks. In Britain too, the tide seemed to be slowly turning against genuflecting, cap-doffing coverage of the rich and famous.

Piers Morgan had been a celebrity reporter himself, editing the showbiz pages of the *Sun* from the age of twenty-four. In the late eighties, celebrities regarded the paper with suspicion and loathing, so Morgan had his work cut out. 'No celebrity would talk to the *Sun*, so I started having to be really nice to them, giving them copy approval, picture retouching, that sort of stuff, just to get them to talk to me. I had to relentlessly lick their arses.' There was a real necessary evil.

From the *Sun*, Morgan was moved across the News

International stable to the *News of the World*, to edit the Sunday newspaper at the age of twenty-nine. The following year he jumped ship from Rupert Murdoch's merry gang to become editor of the *Mirror*. It was a dizzying rise, reflecting his instinctive feel for the culture of the times, which he'd developed on the showbiz beat. At his new paper he hit upon the idea of the 3am girls, three sassy young female reporters who would schmooze the famous in the hope of gaining titbits of unauthorised gossip. The PRs who had previously mediated access between the press and celebrities were written out of the script. Morgan called the girls 'A kind of intellectual Spice Girls. A parody of what showbiz is like now.'

'Piers Morgan wanted to capitalise on ladette culture and massage the ego of male celebrities,' said Jessica Callan, the daughter of a Fleet Street veteran and one of the original trio. 'We don't do PR-led stuff; we do whatever the opposite is . . . Piers can spot a lazy PR handout story a mile off.' So the girls would finagle their way into celebrity bashes – parties for film premières, parties for album launches, parties for sports awards – to snare their unwary prey. However intellectual they might be, the job was really about shoving their tits in celebrities' faces.

The only problem with the 3am girls was that the number of interesting stories they brought in was negligible. They did run a photo of Naomi Campbell leaving anti-drugs counselling and broke the news of this personal struggle, but that only landed them with a writ from the supermodel for invasion of privacy, which led to a court case that the paper lost. And supermodel takes drugs was hardly a world-beating scoop in the first place. Callan said her proudest journalistic moment actually came when Dwight Yorke, a footballer struggling to make it into the first team at Manchester United, asked her at a sporting awards after-show if she would join him in a threesome with his girlfriend, the glamour model Jordan. That was hardly Watergate. On another occasion they led their page with an attack on a music industry PR who had refused to let them come to an end-of-tour party for Kylie Minogue because they had slagged her off. That was a ruthless defence of their hunting ground.

None of this, alas, stopped the girls actually becoming celebrities in their own right. Graydon Carter, the editor of *Vanity Fair*, caught wind of their behaviour and dispatched a writer to London to profile the girls for his newly serious magazine. They were cited as the most desirable role models in the media among students in that discipline in Britain. And *Maxim* magazine judged them the 270th, 271st and 272nd most desirable women in the world. At least this was a view vigorously disputed by Noel Gallagher from the stage at one concert (which sums up where Oasis were at by the turn of this new century), which earned him a volley of abuse in their pages too.

The *Sun* was more friendly to the industry. It meant that its showbiz pages, edited by Dominic Mohan, often lacked a bit of zip, but they landed bigger interviews.

Mohan made that point to the *Vanity Fair* journalist, asking rather pathetically why she wasn't writing a story on him.

It quickly became politic to promote the 3am girls as part of the *Mirror*'s brand. When a male hack discovered that Sven Goran Eriksson was having a fling with his fellow Swede, Ulrika Jonsson, Piers Morgan gave the story to 3am and let this world exclusive run under the girls' byline. Like Sven, who capitalised on his standing as the England football manager by releasing a record of his favourite pieces of music, and like celebrity chef Jamie Oliver, who had recently put out his own *Music To Cook By*, the girls released *The 3am Collection*, an eight-track collection of pop tunes, featuring Kylie among others. It was a shrewd piece of business. 'Certainly we missed a lot of tricks about branding for a long time,' said Morgan. 'I do think the power of the 3am brand is fantastic at the moment . . . Branding is a word that journalists hate, but I've come to quite like it.' This was the man who was also pounding out the message that 'Celebrities have got too big for their boots . . . they need to be taken down a peg or two'. But and what did celebrity involve if not an element of personal branding.

It was inevitable that the girls should be interviewed by *Heat*, the bible of contemporary celebrity culture. The interviewer asked Callan how it felt to have the tables turned on them now that they were as celebrated as the people they wrote about. 'Hard,' she replied, 'because we know that journalists are intrinsically untrustworthy people.' No wonder critics within the profession came to despise them. They weren't the only ones. 'When we go on the red carpet to premières,' Callan continued, 'we get booed sometimes. That's weird.'

It was hard to tell where real life ended and make-believe began, particularly once the girls had themselves entered the narrative of their stories. 'We get to create a living soap opera – people can't wait to find out what happens next,' Callan said.

Of course, Piers Morgan hated *Big Brother* – or at least professed to do so. The *Mirror* was the 'Official *Big Brother* Paper' for the show's second series (they backed Brian; the *Sun* got behind Helen), but for the third it became the 'Official Anti-*Big Brother* Paper'. Dropping the red masthead had made it look more like the more upmarket *Mail*. Now it was starting to think and act like it too – right down to the hypocrisy. In the week before the second series, the *Mirror* ran 17,061 words about *Big Brother* compared to the *Sun*'s 6,664. The equivalent figure a year later was 8,537 words, compared to the *Sun*'s ('No 1 For *Big Brother*') 7,610.

'Our little bunnies are getting frisky,' reported Kevin O'Sullivan, the *Mirror*'s 'Anti-*Big Brother* correspondent', in the second week of the third series. But lest anyone presume he approved of such news, he wrote, 'Put any group of dumb animals in an enclosed environment and before long their thoughts will turn to breeding. And so it was that, with a depressing air of inevitability, the brain-dead residents of Halfwit House spent the weekend jumping into the sack with one another.' And so on and so on for another 600 words. Each day he continued to cover events in the house – disguising his interest with a manufactured sneer.

The coverage of the show remained genuinely enthusiastic in *Heat*. Launched in February 1999 as an entertainment magazine – EMAP, its publishers, thought of it as a British version of the American *Entertainment Weekly* – *Heat* initially struggled to pass the 50,000 circulation mark. Editor Mark Frith, however, slowly tweaked the content, turning the title into a true celebrity magazine and making it more feminine. 'I have a strong idea who the readers are,' he told me. 'And there's a strong part of me that's a twenty-five-year old showbusiness fan from Norwich called Julie.' By the spring of 2002, *Heat* was selling half a million copies, making it the fastest-growing magazine in Europe, comfortably beating its venerable rivals *Hello!*, which clocked in at about the 380,000 mark, and *OK!*, which sold about 320,000 copies, and competing vigorously with the more recent *Now*. It was a crowded and fierce marketplace, but *Heat* made a calculated pitch to appeal to a younger readership. 'The battle between the celebrity weeklies looks set to be between us and *Now*,' Frith said to me when we met. 'We have tapped into the twentysomething market for celebrity and we have got the formula right. The other celeb mags are aimed at your mum or your auntie,' he continued. 'But we have plugged into what younger readers want. *Big Brother* and *Popstars* were phenomenal and we went with that.'

Frith had realised that contemporary show business involved pop and film, as ever, and even the odd stage event (if Madonna or Gwyneth Paltrow were treading the boards in London), but TV was the key to celebrity culture. 'My view is that people are only famous if they're on television,' he said. 'It's the telly and the tabloids that in Britain make people famous. Films? No. Music? No, unless they're on the telly a lot.' *Heat* didn't cover weddings or the lives of minor European royalty, the traditional fare on offer from its older rivals. *OK!* might later learn to blur the line between fact and fiction by devoting a spread to the fictional nuptials of a fictional couple from the fictional *Footballers' Wives*, but *Heat* plunged right on in there, hiring *Big Brother* presenter Davina and then *Big Brother* winner Brian as columnists.

Despite heavy criticism within the industry, Conrad Green, the factual entertainment bloke at the Beeb, went to *Heat* when he was looking to make some new appointments. 'If the best way to find researchers who think in an independent way is to go to a magazine like *Heat*, which has a great understanding of television, then that's where I'll go,' he said defiantly.

I should perhaps reiterate I'm an avid *Heat* reader. It's a magazine of endless fascination, filled with coverage of all the stars I'm interested in, and pitched at quite the perfect tone. The numerous cover lines from the issue that saw the magazine pass the half a million mark for the first time – dated 4–10 May 2002 – tell their own story:

> *Pop Idols* In Love? Gareth and Hayley are secretly dating!
> She finishes with Brum boyfriend
> Their romantic rendezvous
> He tells her 'I love you'
>
> KYLIE
> Exclusive only in *Heat*!
> Her amazingly sexy tour!
>
> ULRIKA
> Heartbroken again!
> Why she bowed out of battle for Sven
>
> DERMOT
> The truth about those gay rumours
>
> EASTENDERS REAL-LIFE DRAMA
> Lucy: 'Steve doesn't love me'
>
> UTTERLY BONKERS!
> Worst-dressed Baftas ever!

And, across the very top of the page: 'POSH and the bump go shopping!' This was a reference to pictures inside of Posh Spice, who was pregnant at the time, going to the shops.

The great thing was, I knew who all those characters were and wanted to read about all of them. Except for the *EastEnders* lot. Mark Frith told me that he could sympathise because he'd only recently become a fan of the show himself. He also said that the Posh story was 'possibly the flimsiest, most tenuous thing we've ever done'.

I visited Frith at the *Heat* offices, just north of Covent Garden in London. QTV, the music channel branded with the title of that other EMAP publication, Q, was playing in the reception area. We talked in an airless office at the back of the building, while he ate his lunch – packed sandwiches. With his enthusiasm for his chosen field of work and understanding of it, he reminded me of Pete Waterman. What he lacked in terms of Waterman's music energy he made up for with his own easy-going charm. And I loved the fact that he was such a real pop fan too. 'I've gone out before and bought the record that's going to be number one the following Sunday to feel part of that excitement,' he said. 'It's really sad, but I bought the Bob The Builder single because I was excited by the idea of Bob The Builder being number one.

'I'm just one of those people who loves a sense of event, and loves a talking point, and loves the thing that everyone else loves.'

It's easy to read *Heat* from cover to cover by the time the bath water is actually still quite tepid and yet no one's claiming that it's anything other than vacuous. But that doesn't mean its readers are stupid. As Frith says: 'We're all intelligent people. We just like to put on our gossip hats once a week and settle down to luxuriate with this magazine. People can separate the serious, worthy stuff from "let's entertain people".' No wonder *Heat*'s slogan was 'the higher the IQ, the greater the need for gossip'. 'If there was any embarrassment about buying the magazine,' said Frith, 'the slogan excuses it; it makes it a magazine you're proud to be seen with.'

Nonetheless, I was often ashamed to be seen picking up a copy of *Heat* at the newsagent's – as if it were one of *OK!* publisher Richard Desmond's other titles or *Loaded*. So that would probably be the shot of me they'd use if, heaven forbid, I were ever to feature in the magazine myself. *Heat*'s guiding principle in its coverage of celebrities was to show them off guard, unkempt, unready, unsanitised. This was the province of the cellulite bottom, the dreaded rogue nipple. '*Heat* features stars in the way we want to see them,' Frith told me, 'which is not up on a pedestal.' Rather down in the gutter. A favourite picture spread of *Heat*'s editor involved Nicole Kidman, world-famous arty actress, very rich thanks to her former husband, leaving a Portaloo. She could be you or me, except she's not. That's funny. It was.

Jennifer Cawthorn was the editor of *Sneak*, a teen spin-off from *Heat* launched by EMAP in May 2002. 'Looking at celebs when they're looking really aspirational is not nearly as exciting as seeing them with their skirt tucked in their knickers,' she said of this boisterous, democratic mindset. 'I think people are increasingly interested in what celebs are really doing,' she continued, 'rather than what the PRs say they are doing. There's so much control of what goes into the media, and teenagers . . . want to know the real story.'

Sneak covered more straight pop than *Heat*, and ran some novel features like Celebrity Cringe, readers' true-life confessions of embarrassing themselves in front of celebrities, like Vanessa from Warrington, who wangled her way backstage at a Blue gig and met Simon, but got an eyelash caught in her eye, which meant her make-up started running down her face and he started looking at her as if she were strange. 'I think he thought I was crying!'

It seemed to me that *Sneak* and *Heat*'s approach was a smarter, funnier, kinder way of dealing with the contemporary celebrity than the *Mirror*'s. But Morgan and his acolytes shared a certain mistrust of the controlling workings of PR. In a world of burgeoning media outlets, the number of real showbiz stars has remained more or less finite. No wonder that those stars can pick and choose who they talk to and which publications they appear in, and make demands for copy approval (or six white chinchillas and a case of Krug in the green room when they do TV chat shows). *Heat*'s geriatric rivals became accustomed to paying ridiculous sums of money to celebs to feature them relaxing in the comfort of their palatial houses or getting hitched.

OK! forked out £300,000 to Kym Marsh to cover her wedding to that bloke from *EastEnders* in the hope of attracting new readers to the magazine. The problem for the magazine was, would those readers stay if they could rely on lots of unauthorised snaps of the *Popstars* and *Pop Idol* and *Big Brother* lot in *Heat* or *Sneak* the following week? After years of attrition, *Hello!* and *OK!* called a truce in their fight with each other, mindful that others were winning the war. When bidding for exclusive photos of Elizabeth Hurley's first child reached £1 million, *Hello!* boss Eduardo Sanchez and *OK!* owner Desmond spoke to each other for the first time in six years, striking a deal to share the costs. (They got the images with a combined bid of £100,000.) It was a trick they repeated for the Beckhams' World Cup send-off party. Phil Hall, *Hello!*'s editor-in-chief, said, 'Big fees do not guarantee good interviews or picture shots – quite the opposite. Money seems to empower publicists to abuse the publications paying their fees.'

Throughout the media, in fact – in the celebrity mags, in the tabs, on the telly – there was a move towards telling the real truth. When Channel 5 ditched its entertainment programme *Exclusive!* and the *Movie Chart Show* in favour of something called *The Edit* in early 2002, the show was produced by the channel's news provider, rather than their entertainment department. At much the same time, BBC Choice's *Liquid News*, a frothy showbiz news show, moved towards programming with a stronger journalistic edge.

This tendency reached its apotheosis on the Internet, which was still like the Wild West in the early twenty-first century. There were plenty of entertainment sites, like Ananova, which did a competent job of rounding up showbiz gossip in the fashion of a proper news agency, but then there was Popbitch, which was more like a furtive rummage round the knicker-drawer of contemporary culture. The Popbitch site was built around message boards on which anyone – though it helped if you were in the media or music industry – could post rumours or comments about pop stars or pop culture or life in general, and a weekly e-mail picking out the juiciest gossip. It was the e-mail that got me hooked, but then I graduated to checking the message boards on an almost hourly basis in the course of a working day. Inevitably, 95 per cent of the postings – by my strict mathematical calculation – were pointless, little more than aimless chat passed between members of the in-crowd. I never posted anything myself, partly because I just didn't think I'd understand how to (as a founder of the local Luddite chapter), partly because the gossip I did have was far too scandalous ever to be published (possibly). But others did come up with the goods, and it soon became evident that lots of journalists on respectable publications were confirmed Popbitchers – by which I mean that some of them probably posted on it and all of them read it. Popbitch broke the news that Posh Spice was pregnant with her second child, a story which appeared in the tabloids a couple of days later. And when there was a story on the message board that Mr Posh had done a merchandising deal with Marks and Spencer, the *Financial Times* picked it up for its next day's edition.

Part of the appeal of Popbitch was that it was an entirely anonymous operation. The identity of the people posting information was always disguised by an alias. Only a search at Companies House revealed that Popbitch's two directors were Neil Stevenson, a former deputy editor of *Heat* and the new editor of *The Face*, and Camilla Wright, his girlfriend. When Stevenson took up his post at *The Face* in early 2002, the pioneering style and youth culture magazine was in dire straits, selling only about 55,000 copies a month, compared to a mid-nineties peak of more than 100,000. It seemed that even the arbiters of modern cool had been overwhelmed by the explosion of pop culture and phenomena such as Popbitch.

'*The Face* has lost touch,' Stevenson said. 'The world has changed a lot in recent years. The amount of pop culture has increased, television channels have gone from four to two hundred, there's the Web and e-mail and mobile phones – people are overwhelmed by pop culture. And *The Face* has got to deal with the fact that people have a lot more choice and a lot less time.'

Of course, it wasn't just *The Face* that was in trouble. The *NME*'s fiftieth birthday celebrations in the spring of 2002 were muted by the news that its number of readers had fallen to a sorry 70,000 – 47,000 down on 1996 and 230,000 down on the mid-sixties. But the difference between now and then wasn't simply the Web and e-mail; it was also the fact that there were more music titles now, each targeting a niche in the market, and more general publications – from *Heat* to *FHM* plus the broadsheets – covering music in some shape or form as well. The music press no longer had a monopoly on pop and pop culture. According to Barney Hoskyns, a staff writer for the *NME* in the early eighties and latterly the editor of rocksbackpages.com, a website archiving great rock journalism: 'Music in all popular culture has become diffuse. It doesn't have the same kind of tribal power. You can read about pop in any kind of magazine. Wherever you find it, there's a uniformity of approach and style. You get everything served up in easily digestible pieces.

'I think there is an exhaustion among readers,' Hoskyns continued. 'The rock press keeps trying to build new things up into legitimate movements but the response is one of indifference. Writing itself has diminished in value. There is so much text coming at us from all directions that readers really don't care any more.'

In December 2000, *Melody Maker* bit the dust, a few weeks short of its seventy-fifth birthday, and was nominally folded into the *NME*. By this time it was pumping the greater part of its resources into its online version. In America, meanwhile, Jan Wenner finally stepped down from editing the increasingly feeble *Rolling Stone* (after doing weird things, like reviewing Mick Jagger's most recent album himself, and giving it the very rare *RS* accolade of five stars; the record still sold like shit, though). In his place, they brought in someone called Ed Needham, the bloke who had turned *FHM* into the market leader in men's mags in Britain. Needham planned fewer of the epic pieces of rock reporting and investigative journalism that *Rolling Stone* had pioneered, promising to introduce shorter, bittier articles. Jan Wenner could see his point. 'There is so much media around,' he said. 'Back when *Rolling Stone* was publishing these seven-thousand-word stories, there was no CNN, no Internet. And now you can travel around the globe, and you don't need these long stories to get up to speed.'

As if I cared about *Rolling Stone*! If I bought any rock title, it was *Mojo*, founded in the mid-nineties for people like me who wanted to read 70,000-word articles on the sort of acts that *Rolling Stone* had first championed. But by this time I was exclusively reading *Heat* for my weekly fix of happenings and on-goings in contemporary culture.

Was it the real culture? That depends on how you define reality and your observation of the modern condition. In the week after 11 September, *Heat* ran a spread on how the terrorist strikes had affected the world of entertainment, leading their Hot off the Press pages with a snap of Britney Spears getting off a plane in Australia in tears at the news. At *Hello!*, editor Phil Hall, an old newspaper hand, instead decided to report on the terrorist attacks and their terrifying aftermath.

'I am now of the view that we shouldn't have done

as much as we did,' Mark Frith said to me. 'Our view should have been, "This is not a celebrity story and people want a safe enclave from the horrible things that are happening and want to be entertained".'

'I wouldn't patronise people by covering 11 September,' he continued. 'I don't really have anything to offer on it. We have a role. We didn't know if people still wanted us in the role after the attacks. Sales wavered for two weeks ... and then continued their upward pattern.'

6

THE BIRTH OF OUR POP PHENOMENON

'There's nothing negative about crisps, do you know what I mean?' – Ginger Spice

'In an ideal world it would be great if everyone knew who Simon Fuller was,' Simon Fuller once said, 'but didn't know what I looked like – like Egon Ronay. How cool would that be?'

Far be it from me to say, but a restaurant critic for role model? Noting the Coasters and Frankie Avalon CDs on the shelf in his office, another interviewer identified 'an endearing whiff of ballroom-dancer naffness' about him. That seemed strange for a forty-one-year-old who came of age at the time of punk. Yet this is the man who transformed the modern pop industry.

If Pete Waterman's records had scarred my youth through their ubiquity, The Spice Girls and S Club 7 threatened to put me off pop music for life. There were some great singles – 'Wannabe' for example; even I could recognise that. But everything else became about branding and marketing. There was a Spice Girls film and an S Club TV show and endless merchandising, all aggressively pitched at the kids. In fact, after S Club 7 came S Club Juniors. Fuller would soon be after my children too.

The funny thing, however, was that Fuller's acts epitomised the trends that were killing the music industry – this was the triumph of the men in suits – but tended to sell millions and were rare success stories in beleaguered times. 'I just love moments of time,' Fuller once said. 'The Monkees were crap, really, but you look at it, and it takes you back to the 1960s. And I would like to think that shows like S Club will capture this moment, as The Spice Girls captured theirs.'

Simon Fuller was the grandson of a music-hall comic and acrobat and was always interested in the entertainment business. 'It would be great to be able to say Simon was this Machiavellian monster who terrorised the fourth form,' said a former school friend from Hastings Grammar, 'but he was just very likeable.' Nonetheless, there were early signs of an entrepreneurial streak: he ran the school music club and managed a class-mate's band. Instead of going to university, he started running local discos.

In 1983 Fuller was working as a publishing scout for Chrysalis Records when he heard Madonna's 'Holiday' and pushed the company to sign her. The singer was unknown at the time, and Chrysalis decided to pass, though they did at least hire the writers of the track. Two years later this latest Mr Pop set up his own management company. His first act was synthesiser whizz Paul Hardcastle, who had a catchy track about the Vietnam War. (That was a very eighties kind of thing; I went off the Human League when they came out with 'The Lebanon'.) Under Fuller's guidance, the song went to number one here – and in twelve other countries – and won the Ivor Novello award for the best-selling single of 1985. The company took its name from its title: 19.

Unlike great rock managers of the past – the Peter Grants and Malcolm McLarens of this world – Fuller was a considerate soul who placed great emphasis on loyalty to his clients. Years later Paul Hardcastle contributed music to the S Club 7 project. In the late eighties Fuller picked up pop singer Cathy Dennis and shrewdly stuck by her when she turned to a career in songwriting. In 1990 he started managing Annie Lennox when the Eurythmics split and helped turn her into an international solo star. At the final of *Pop Idol*, she was in the audience.

In March 1995, Fuller took charge of a fledgling girl group that he called The Spice Girls. 'He's like a wise little Buddha,' Ginger later said of him. 'You hear so many stories about how inhumane a lot of managers are and I just think, God, thank you.' (Later, of course, Geri Halliwell became a leading authority on matters of spirituality.)

The Spice Girls sold 21 million albums under Fuller and became one of the most famous pop bands in history. But when he started working with them, the potential wasn't obvious. 'I consciously, methodically did my homework for weeks,' he later said. Fuller figured that girls didn't buy records by girl groups because girls groups were invariably too sexy and threatening. A gang to which you'd want to belong was far more like it. 'And everything they do has got to be marketed along those lines.'

But Fuller's work didn't stop there. The Spice Girls broke the mould for the way in which pop groups did business. The revenue they generated was partly built on record sales, but the real moolah came from sponsorship and advertising. The Girls struck deals with Pepsi, Walker's crisps, Channel 5, Impulse deodorant, Asda supermarkets, Polaroid cameras, Cadbury chocolate bars, Chupa Chups sweets, Unilever fragrance and Sony video games. They could probably have helped the Pope sell condoms.

The people at Pepsi were initially against their deal because they wanted to attract the hip and happening seventeen- to twenty-four-year-olds who would never like The Spice Girls. Fuller thought this idiotic because all seventeen-year-olds are interested in is 'getting pissed and shagging'. 'What do they care about Pepsi?' he asked rhetorically. 'You want six-year-olds to identify with Pepsi. Global branding works like that. Why do adults drink Ribena? Because they drank it as kids and they love it. That's clear cut. It's amazing how big companies haven't figured it out.'

Fuller surrounded himself with people who understood that the blatant branding that was previously the preserve of movie studios and burger chains could be applied to anything. The marketing brains who had seen Manchester United's product profits soar from £5 to £28 million in the mid-nineties, for example, came aboard. Paul Conroy, the man who signed The Spice

Girls to Virgin, said: 'The way things work now is that marketing and A&R move hand in hand. We ask, can the company create something the company can sell? Does the singer and the song have what it takes to make a hit? How much impact will the artist make on TV? Extraordinarily, until very recently none of those questions was ever asked, it was just the A&R department choosing what music they liked.'

What about the girls themselves? They seemed happy. Ginger certainly wasn't bothered about branding: 'There's nothing negative about crisps, do you know what I mean?'

Yet in November 1997, on the night of ITV's *An Audience with The Spice Girls* special, the group sacked Fuller. The issue seemed to be who really ran the band, but relations had grown strained when Fuller started dating Baby Spice. Either way, a pay-off of between £15 and £20 million surely softened the blow. The people who really suffered were of course the Girls themselves. Without the guidance of Mr Bouffant Hairdo, the good ship Spice quickly foundered. Geri quit, records flopped, and babies were born.

Grown-ups can't play at being kiddie pop stars for ever. Or if they do they end up like Michael Jackson. Either that or their fans outgrow them.

As PR guru Max Clifford, who first made his name in the music business in the sixties, said at the time: 'I've seen this happen fifty times. It never works out well for the artist. Groups like Take That and The Spice Girls have only a limited shelf life. They have one or two years to blaze away and make the most of what they are doing before they're finished. The fact is that little girls, who make up the majority of their audience, grow up.

'Fuller is a hot property. He's the one who had the vision to make it work – who made them stars. He'll have the pick of all the up-and-coming acts. In ten years no one will give a damn about The Spice Girls, but Fuller will still be in business.'

Five years later Not-So-Baby Spice signed up with him again. Posh and even Geri discussed the possibilities of working together once more. To Fuller's credit, he bore no grudges.

That didn't mean he didn't have bigger fish to fry by that time. The day after his pact with The Spice Girls fell apart, he sat down to plan a band. Or brand, if you prefer.

To find the seven members of S Club Fuller spent an estimated £1 million auditioning 10,000 kids. (The *Popstars* judges saw 1,000.) To no one's surprise all bar one of the eventual successful applicants had some sort of stage school experience. 'We wanted maybe two who had really good voices, two who could dance, one who was into fashion, one who was the big brother figure,' PR man Julian Henry later recalled. Marketing deals with Pepsi, Cadbury, Hasbro and BT quickly followed. Soon you could buy S Club singing dolls, keyrings, mouse mats, pencil cases and stationery.

A website was launched, at the cost of about £6 million, promising to take the concept of the fan club to a new level. To be an official 'S Clubber' you had to register with the site, which involved revealing your name, age and what part of the country you came from (building useful data for the money men). Within two years 120,000 members were receiving e-mails and text messages on their mobiles giving updates and gossip on the group.

The real secret of S Club 7's success, however, was surprisingly old-fashioned. Fuller had toyed with launching The Spice Girls like The Monkees with a TV series, but by the time a deal for a twenty-six-part series was on the table, the timing was off. Fuller settled instead for a movie, *Spice World*, a semi-fictionalised account of the Girls' rise, written by his brother, closely aping the early Beatles flicks.

When it came to S Club, it was back to Plan A.

'I thought, I haven't been doing this for however long I've been doing this to still be waiting for this TV show or that radio station to like our single,' Fuller later recalled. 'There's got to be a better way of breaking bands.'

In April 1999 *Miami 7* aired. It followed the wacky adventures of S Club 7 on their quest to find fame and fortune in America.

Henry's House took the teen media – *Top of the Pops* magazine, *Smash Hits*, *TV Hits* – out to Miami to publicise the show for the BBC. The grown-up press weren't invited. The show quickly picked up viewing figures of 3.5 million. When the first S Club 7 single was released at the end of the series in June 1999, it went straight to number one. A second series followed, called *LA7*, along with a series of one-off specials. By this time the seven plucky pop kids had been seen by 90 million viewers in 110 countries.

Like *SpiceWorld*, which featured Richard E. Grant hamming up the role of the Girls' manager Clifford, the TV series featured lots of self-deprecating humour. Even an ageing rock fan could be tickled by episode three of the third series, *Hollywood 7*, called 'Public Relations'. The S Club's hapless (fictional) manager hires a PR to make the band famous by involving them in a series of scandals. One of the lads has to date a teen pop star. Two of the girls go on a Jerry Springer-style TV show; a third gets caught up in a plastic surgery mishap. And so on and so on. Only in this fantasy world, in the end, the PR gets the boot.

In real life the scandals started soon enough.

There were stories in December 2000 that the group had threatened to split up after working a succession of eighteen-hour days and travelling economy class back from a promotional tour to Spain. What was more, a money-spinning deal with BT for the S Club concept had apparently netted the band members nothing more than a free mobile with thirty minutes of free talk time. I've never owned a mobile in my life, but I could sort of see S Club's point. Polydor quickly wrote them cheques of £100,000 as an early Christmas present.

The following March, Bradley, Jon and Paul threatened to bring the whole edifice crashing down when they were arrested in Covent Garden for possession of a small amount of cannabis. Quaker Oats pulled out of a Sugar Puffs sponsorship deal and the Labour Party dropped the idea of using the single 'Reach' as an election anthem (this was the same Labour Party that subsequently gave the green light to getting high). BT and Cadbury's said they were 'extremely disappointed' and 'would never condone the use of drugs'. Fuller rode the storm out, issuing a statement that the band were 'gutted' to have let their fans down, but Paul had had enough. Plans were announced that he would leave and start again in a nu metal outfit featuring his real mates.

But even if the band was in trouble, the brand was still strong. In April 2002, Fuller launched the diffusion range: S Club Juniors.

There had always been a lot of bands aimed at the pre-teen market, from The Monkees and The Archies onwards, but by this stage in pop's evolutionary history there were also plenty of bands comprising kids who hadn't known puberty. The charts were threatened by acts such as Kaci – described on Popbitch as an 'ambitious Florida poptart with the smile of an angel and the coldly ambitious eyes of a Moscow prostitute' – and French strumpet Alizee, as well as Britney's younger sister Jamie Lynn Spears.

Following the success on TV of *Popstars*, GMTV launched *Totstars*, a talent search for children aged between five and eleven who competed against each other to try to win a recording contract with Universal and a place at a stage school. The judges included TV presenter Claire Sweeney (whose public profile had been transformed by her appearance on *Celebrity Big Brother* in 2001) and the former manager of juvenile opera singer Charlotte Church.

It all stirred distant memories from my childhood of the *Mini-Pops* phenomenon in which wee bairns were dressed up like their favourite pop stars for the telly. The shows were first broadcast at prime time on the new and supposedly highbrow Channel 4 in 1982. The children also made a series of albums, covering the chart hits of the day. I looked for some info on them on the Web and found a couple of fan nostalgia sites. I am probably being tracked by the paedophile division of Interpol.

If that was disturbing, S Club Juniors were something else again. There were supposed to be seven members, to complement their adult counterparts, but after four open auditions in which 10,000 children were whittled down to fourteen, S Club 7 themselves were asked to make the final casting call. They bottled their decision and let eight stay in the group, all aged between eleven and fourteen.

On the website and in their own mini-magazine, there were helpful descriptions of who was who. Perhaps anxious to avoid the problems of S Club Paul, thirteen-year-old Calvin was already billed as a 'nu metal nutter'. His 'favourite pop band' was Linkin Park. Best school subject? PE. Worst? Maths.

Of course, 19 were careful to reassure the public that the kids were being looked after properly, saying they were working closely with the children's parents and local councils to ensure the group were able to maintain the required amount of schooling. While recording away from home, the eight of them had two chaperones and a tutor. 'We're being extremely stringent about their academic studies,' said Nicki Chapman.

I caught a bit of the nurturing process on a BBC children's series which followed the group's creation. 'The girls love being made up,' said the voice-over. 'But sometimes beauty hurts.' Cut to a shot of a stylist savagely plucking the youngsters' eyebrows. Another one of the children said: 'We prove that you don't have to go to school to be successful.' Michelle Elliott, director of child protection charity Kidscape, was not impressed, claiming the concept exploited the children. 'We all know what happens – they get burned out. I hope this fails . . . it's disgusting.'

In April 2002 the band released their first single, 'One Step Closer' (another Cathy Dennis number). I hate to say it but it sounded pretty good to me, although – alas – a new girl off *Neighbours* pipped them to number one.

Despite this blip and industry gloom, Fuller's acts were huge successes and seemed to disprove the notion that marketing was the wrong way forward. The funny thing was, I even preferred them to their contemporaries like Boyzone and later Blue or Five. There was an enjoyable buzz there.

Perhaps this was pop done properly, even if that meant treating pop like any other commodity. One of Fuller's old allies is Julian Henry, a former music journalist, who founded Henry's House in April 1998 with Fuller as one of its three directors. Their first clients were S Club 7, and a soft drink brand, Tango. Henry regarded both parties in much the same way.

'People relate to talent and consumer brands in similar ways,' he told the *Financial Times*. 'The most successful celebrities are marketed as brands ... The needs of a celebrity will be different to that of a brand, but the principles for the communication work tend to be the same.' The company later dealt with TV personalities such as Johnny Vaughan and Jamie Theakston, as well as Absolut vodka, the mobile phone network Orange, and magazines including *The Face* and *FHM*.

Significantly, however, 19 was an atypical operation. When *Pop Idol* was finished, right-on comedian Ben Elton took the opportunity to join the bandwagon, attacking the phenomenon (while publicising *We Will Rock You*, the musical he had written with Queen). According to Elton, young people today are being culturally disenfranchised. 'What they wear, what they watch, what they listen to, even what they eat is being planned years in advance by colossal global corporations whose economies of scale dictate that they sell everything to everybody at the same time and then start over again the following week,' he wrote in the *Daily Mail*.

All that sounded fairly convincing, even if his argument was poleaxed by citing Noddy Holder as the kind of talent the industry was failing to produce in its preference for Wills or Gareths. But really it was utter nonsense because 19 is nothing like a colossal global corporation. Fuller and his team generated all the ideas and concepts themselves. Record companies were principally used as service providers. He'd brand and bring them a product, and they'd put up the front and money (and manufacture the bleedin' discs). With The Spice Girls, Simon Fuller worked with Virgin, a subsidiary of EMI. With S Club 7 he teamed up with Universal. For *Pop Idol*, the deals were with BMG. These were the biggest pop acts of the last decade but they weren't the product of major-label thinking.

'We don't want twenty people being involved in every decision,' Fuller said. 'Corporations are about taking weeks, months to make decisions. I can act in two seconds – my decision is final and it happens. That makes us faster and more effective than our competition.'

When the majors seized control of the industry in the early nineties the majority of independent labels sold up or sold out. But for the smartest operators, the rise of the conglomerates could be good news. While the big beasts locked horns and crashed around the valley floor, there were plenty of pickings to be had at ground level.

'The majors are so focused on profit,' Ajax Scott from *Music Week* said, 'that independents can go to new acts and say, "Don't sign with these money-obsessed idiots who do everything at a snail's pace . . . we're funkier and we're faster."'

True enough. There may not have been too many Ahmet Erteguns out there, but labels such as the fully independent Domino could be relied upon to find the interesting talent that the majors had missed in their search for acts that were plainly marketable.

It wasn't just independents nipping at the majors' ankles. In California, Beck, Courtney Love, The Eagles, Sheryl Crow and a number of other big draws campaigned for new legislation to overturn repressive labour laws that held musicians to seven-album deals. Wacko Jacko called on civil rights activist the Reverend Al Sharpton to state his case, who said, 'Economic servitude, no matter how comfortable the slave is, is still slavery.'

Even the *Wall Street Journal* came in on their side. 'For all the twenty-first century glitz that surrounds it,' the paper sounded, 'the popular music business is distinctly medieval in character: the last form of indentured servitude.'

One of the plucky citizens fighting the evil empire was Britain's own George Michael, who with Robbie Williams was really our only recognisable pop idol before *Pop Idol*'s babies were born. I'd warmed to George since learning that he'd turned into a heavy dope smoker to make his last album (though I've never heard it). When he was ready to make his latest comeback in the early part of 2002, he made a one-single deal with Universal, figuring that an artist of his stature should hold the whip hand in negotiations. If the company got behind the record and helped make it a success, he'd let them have his new long-player. If they didn't do the job, he would look elsewhere. It was only a pity that 'Freeek!' – with its video featuring whips and chains – peaked at number seven in its week of release. Straight in ahead of it was Gareth Gates, with his cover of 'Unchained Melody'.

19 wasn't a record label, however, or a beleaguered artist (here is the answer to their worries: make some good records). It was a think tank, churning out ideas, dreaming dreams, and helping them be realised. During The Spice Girls madness Fuller had fewer than a dozen people working for him, but by the time *Pop Idol* was on the boil he employed around sixty experts covering different fields, including TV, music management, music publishing, recording, artist/writer and producer management, sponsorship and promotion. 19 had developed into the privately owned 19 Group, an umbrella organisation binding ten separate companies such as 19TV together.

Nicki Chapman was 19 Management's creative director, and Nigel Lythgoe left his £200,000-a-year job at LWT to establish the TV company. Charles Garland arrived from advertising agency Bartle Bogle Hegarty to run the marketing division, while Richard Eyre, the former head of ITV, Capital Radio and Pearson TV, came on board in a non-executive role. It was a bit like *The Magnificent Seven*, the way Fuller assembled the team, or that Kurosawa movie.

Perhaps most alarmingly, Fuller did all this for fun. 'He's a real enthusiast,' Ajax Scott told me. 'He's always so busy developing new ideas for packing mass market entertainment that it's easy to forget that he's really into music. But he'll scamper round his office saying, "Oh, you've got to hear this!"

'Over the years his acts have released some great pop – though that said, he'll always be remembered for producing pop phenomena rather than pop songs.'

In the future all music companies might work a bit like 19. The rise of the Internet's file-swapping culture combined with the vertical integration of multi-media conglomerates has encouraged a situation in which the big boys' principal business could become the exploitation of copyright across a range of media. Other people would deal in the business of finding and developing talent.

Fuller seemed to be positioning himself for just such an eventuality when he told the *Financial Times* that he would never float 19, 'but I'd like to have a trade partner – an entertainment-based company that would give me the scale to push my ideas to their ultimate conclusion'. In all likelihood, according to this scenario, record companies would become huge distribution companies that acquired copyrights for exploitation, then distributed them through electronic means.

In fact, as Pete Waterman has said, recorded copyright will become less important. Songs will be the future of record companies' income. Record companies will effectively become publishers, making money by charging a small fee each time someone copies a recording from the Internet, or listens to it on digital TV. That is exactly the way music publishers earned their corn before record companies took over the industry in the mid-fifties.

'Simon Fuller's success reflects the way in which the business is changing,' said Ajax Scott, 'and it points up what the potential is for those who can see beyond the traditional business model. Simon Fuller isn't screwing the business. You could say that more people should be doing what he's doing.'

The strange thing was, after fifty years, the business was really turning full circle.

7

THE BIRTH OF POP CULTURE

'The staple sound is an animal expression of joy – half shriek, half sigh' – Picture Post

It is usually assumed that pop culture began in Britain in 1956 with the arrival at cinemas of *Rock around the Clock*, the first real rock and roll feature film. Either then or two years later when Cliff Richard scored a number-two hit with 'Move It', the first real British rock and roll record.

How nice to see Sir Cliff on Jonathan Ross's TV talk show in early 2002, promoting his latest single. 'Pop music hasn't really changed at all,' he said. 'We try to compartmentalise it and call it ga-raage.' Cue titters from the audience. 'But it's still pop or rock'n'roll.' Spot on.

Yet before there was Cliff, there were others. It's impossible to claim that this generation of romantic crooners such as Dennis Lotis, Frankie Vaughan, David Whitfield and Dickie Valentine are the unsung heroes of home-grown rock and roll. I should know; I've listened to the records in the painful course of dutiful research. But the long history of British pop culture needs to give them prominence. 'When they first appear on the stage – any music-hall stage in England – a flashing smile visible above the inevitable midnight blue "uniform", you must sit in the gallery to learn what popularity means in 1954,' Robert Muller of the *Picture Post* wrote that year, describing these first pop idols.

'They are mostly young girls up there, splashing in a crazy pool of adoration. Usually, they are "unescorted", sitting hunched forward, eager little hands squashing shiny faces, half-open mouths emitting a strange, a continuous symphony of sound. The staple sound is an animal expression of joy – half shriek, half sigh. And the shrieks are bridged by a humming noise, accompanied by hugging movements, as if a running motor were waiting for the accelerator to be pressed down – by a remembered note of music, or a word, from the singer on the stage. And when the song is ended, the arms go into action, flapping and tearing the air. Hands are whipped together. And above the shrieks, and the moans, and the sighs, you hear the frenzied appeals: "Oh, Frankie!"; "Oh, Dickie!"; "Oh—!"'

The dominant style of music at the time was big band swing. In 1951 there were 450 Mecca and Locarno dance halls in Britain, as well as thousands of assembly halls and hotel ballrooms licensed for dancing. A typical palais might offer dancing six afternoons and evenings a week, with live music and soft drinks. Teenagers didn't get much of a look-in. Indeed, many dance halls catered only for the over-fifties, and in many there were signs banning jiving, lest anyone get too carried away.

In November 1952, however, the fledgling *New Musical Express* published the first-ever record sales chart – which seems as good a place as any from which to date the birth of the British music industry. The first number one was 'Here In My Heart' by Al Martino, a twenty-five-year-old American who kept the top spot for the next eight weeks. His main rival and the top chart act of 1952 was Vera Lynn, the forces' sweetheart, who clocked up four Top 10 hits in the same period. (Martino soon faded from view, before appearing as the Mafia-owned nightclub singer in *The Godfather*, which prepared the ground for a Top 5 hit in 1973 with 'Spanish Eyes', his second million-seller.)

Neither of these two could be considered a force for social insurrection. Nor could a song such as David Whitfield's 1954 version of 'Cara Mia', to take one example, which bears scant resemblance to 'Street Fighting Man' or 'Smack My Bitch Up'. It was a number-one record for a staggering ten weeks, selling over 3.5 million copies, and the song also reached the US Top 10, a rare feat for a British singer at the time. Listening to it now, with its syrupy backing vocals and cheap sentiments, it seems astonishing that teenage girls once swooned over the singer. Yet swoon and scream they did.

Alongside our own brigade of Brylcreemed boys such as Whitfield and Dickie Valentine, there was also a handful of young(ish) American heart-throbs, who picked up where their GI forebears left off in the affections of young British females. Chief among them was former cowboy saddle-maker Guy Mitchell, who regularly toured Britain in the fifties, appearing at the London Palladium for the first time in 1952, and Johnnie Ray, who enjoyed his first British hit the same year.

The Prince of Wails, the Howling Success, the Nabob of Sob – Ray is the only one of these fifties singers I can listen to with any sense of real pleasure, and he has been hailed by the likes of Bob Dylan as the true link between the staid ballad singing of the fifties and rock and roll. It helps that Ray's life itself was a real sob story. Deaf in his right ear from the age of twelve, he struggled for years to make it as a singer in Hollywood, before finally bursting to number one in the US charts in 1951 with the wonderfully dramatic 'Cry'. Ray was heavily influence by black gospel and R&B acts such as The Prisonaires. He was also haunted by allegations of homosexuality and drug-taking, and later achieved more success in Europe and Australia than in the States. He had his first hit in Britain in 1952, followed by three number ones. Pete Waterman remembers listening to Ray's 'Just Walkin' In The Rain' as a young child because 'it was different to anything I'd heard at home, because my dad was a Deanna Durbin fan and it didn't sound anything like that'.

The singer himself once described a more immediate effect on his young fans in this country. 'They would smash automobiles and stage doors and everything else. It was not uncommon for little girls to fall down and for other fans to step on them trying to get to me. What amused me more was the press. They were sending psychiatrists into the audience to try to analyse why people were so hysterical.' In May 1955 the *Sunday Pictorial* had run a feature headlined: 'Is Johnnie Ray a mass hypnotist?'. The author identified Ray's USP – 'He cries like a peeler in a onion-soup factory ... his tears have the potency of pure nitro-glycerine' – before calling on the magazine's resident 'Bobby-Sox Doctor, a distinguished medical man' for his thoughts on the make-up of the audience.

'His fans ... are mainly young people who feel they are tiny cogs in a huge machine, people who live from pay day to pay day,' he commented. 'In the main, they are sufferers from the 20th-century complaint – Suburban Blues. Their employers think of them as "hands". They are growing up in a society which is failing to integrate the lives of us all.'

Well, maybe there was some truth in that. I guess it's hard to think your way back into the hardship and turmoil of post-war Britain from the cosseted vantage point of the next century – like they say in hip hop, I'm not feeling it. But after the fighting came a huge process of reconstruction, signalled by Labour's victory over Churchill in the 1946 election and pieces of legislation like the 1944 Education Act, which was implemented two years later.

One reading of that Act, which introduced a system

of secondary schooling from the age of eleven for every child in the country, posits that within the course of a generation it transformed Britain into a true meritocracy dependent on talent. Certainly in the long term that view stands up – though clearly the recent success of celebrities with no discernible talent calls for some tinkering with the theory. But to teenagers in Britain in the late forties, the new law seemed to enshrine the class system: middle-class children went to grammar school while the grubby urchins from down the road trooped off to secondary moderns. The future looked the colour of porridge for the majority of young Britons.

Yet the fifties was an optimistic, sunny decade, whatever the views of old crusties like the great shaman of cultural criticism, T.S. Eliot. 'There is no doubt that in our headlong rush to educate everybody, we are lowering our standards,' he wrote. '[We are] destroying our ancient edifices to make ready the ground upon which the barbarian nomads of the future will encamp in their mechanised caravans.'

Back in the real world, a new wave of economic prosperity kick-started a consumer boom, which brought domestic appliances and electrical goods into working-class homes for the first time. To take one example, the number of TV licence-holders shot up from under 14,000 in 1947 to over 750,000 in 1951. The Coronation in 1953 (following the young Queen's accession to the throne in '52) was seen by more than 20 million people on 2.7 million sets. Ten and a half million people owned TV sets in 1960.

Newspapers and contemporary films like 1956's *My Teenage Daughter* expressed a routine anti-Americanism, but the country was growing more American by the day. Indeed, the very concept of the teenager – an American invention of the previous decade – was now born in Britain. Young people suddenly had money in their pockets. By 1959, when a pamphlet called *The Teenager Consumer* was published, there was 'a grand total of £900 millions a year to be spent by teenagers at their own discretion'. Even though unmarried people under the age of twenty-five were included in this definition of teenagers, *in real terms* this was twice the pre-war figure.

In 1960 British teens spent £850 million, which was only 5 per cent of the national spend, but included 40 per cent of the record players, 30 per cent of the cosmetics and toiletries and 28 per cent of cinema tickets. And the post-war baby boom meant there were 800,000 more teenagers in the population in 1963 than there had been a decade before.

Before the war, people in their teenage years dressed and acted like adults. (Today, of course, lots of adults dress as if they've just turned thirteen.) In the fifties they set about creating their own identity. For inspiration the young working classes looked to the wartime spiv, in his zoot suit and kipper tie; abroad to Americans, a glimpse of whom some had had through contact with the servicemen stationed in the country since 1942 (who brought nylons –

and-their own radio stations playing the occasional R&B record); and upwards, to the toffs of the time. Pupils at Eton in the thirties and young men about town in the forties started instructing their tailors on Savile Row to cut their suits in the Edwardian manner with long jackets, narrow trousers and velvet collars. Slowly, working-class lads from south of the river began copying the look. It was an assertion of their new-found personal wealth – it might cost £100 to assemble the full uniform – just as black American kids started buying Tommy Hilfiger's preppie clothes as a mark of status back in the day when hip hop was blowing up.

The Teddy boys that emerged were usually perceived as hooligans, as the benefit of fifty years of scare-mongering about pop culture would lead us to expect. In fact, from 1950 to 1955 juvenile crimes dropped year on year.

In '55, however, there was well-publicised trouble when Richard Brooks' film *The Blackboard Jungle* hit cinema screens. This 'shock story of today's high school hoodlums' didn't feature any music, but 'Rock Around The Clock' by Bill Haley and the Comets played over the end credits. After screenings there were reports of Teddy boy riots throughout south London. The shrewd men of Hollywood capitalised on this furore a year later by releasing a movie called *Rock around the Clock*. A highly fictionalised account of the discovery of rock and roll in America by a small-time promoter, who visits a small town to find

Bill Haley and the Comets packing in the crowds, it quickly attracted controversy. On 10 September 1955, the *Manchester Guardian* reported that a screening was stopped for eighteen minutes in the hope that the uproar among the 900-strong audience would subside. Each time one of the rock and roll bands interrupted the narrative, however, 'boys leapt from the front stalls into the front aisle and stamped their suede shoes in the octopus whirling of jive.

'Young people at the back of the cinema . . . gave vent to their emotion by stretching their arms out to the screen like savages drunk with coconut wine at a tribal sacrifice . . . Even two usherettes were seen tapping their hands against the chocolate trays.' Two days later the rioting spread to the streets following a showing of the film in south London which prompted watch committees in other towns and cities to ban it.

In 1956, Princess Margaret went to see the Jayne Mansfield vehicle *The Girl Can't Help It*, the story of a gangster who hires a down-and-out press agent to turn his blonde bimbo of a girlfriend into a recording star. When Little Richard and Gene Vincent sang on screen, HRH was reported to have tapped her stockinged feet on the brass rail of the royal circle.

In September of that year, *The Times* had told its readers of a strange new star on the horizon, 'a raw young Southerner, Mr Elvis Presley, now only 21, whose combination of a hill-billy style of wailing with bodily contortions that are supposed to suggest the "fundamental human drive" took him even beyond the peaks of popularity enjoyed most recently by the tearful Mr Johnny [sic] Ray and Mr Frank Sinatra'.

So much for the notion that the Thunderer only got groovy in the late sixties when they bigged up Mick Jagger. But in fact the paper wasn't first with the news. 'Heartbreak Hotel' had actually entered the British hit parade in May, reaching number two and staying in the charts for the next twenty weeks. Cliff Richard later recalled hearing the record for the first time. 'I thought, God – *this* is what I want to do.'

Cliff became the country's most famous Elvis impersonator, but Tommy Steele got there first. Tommy Hicks was on two weeks' leave from his job as a merchant seaman when he hooked up with his friends Lionel Bart and Mike Pratt to play some skiffle. This was the latest craze – a home-grown, cheaper version of rock and roll, stylistically different but in essence much the same. The trio were soon discovered by a young New Zealand entrepreneur named John Kennedy in the famous 2i's coffee bar in Soho. Hicks changed his name to Steele, and with Kennedy's help landed a gig at the Condor Club. There he met the man who can plausibly claim to have invented British pop and rock and roll – Larry Parnes.

Parnes – a hugely influential figure much admired both by Malcolm McLaren, the man who managed The Sex Pistols, and Pete Waterman, producer of Kylie Minogue – was born in Willesden in north-east London in 1930. His uncle was a pre-war music-hall performer called Len Young the Singing Fool, and by the age of eight he was organising his first show, featuring a group of children. Two years after leaving school at the age of sixteen, he was running his own women's clothing shops in Romford, Essex.

One evening a friend took him to a bar in the West End of London called La Caverne, which Parnes ended up buying. The venue was a hang-out for theatrical agents and producers. Parnes then invested in a play called *The House of Shame*. It was losing money hand over fist until John Kennedy, its new publicist, changed the name to *Women of the Streets* and persuaded two actresses to stand outside the theatre during the interval dressed as whores. The girls were promptly arrested, leading to newspaper headlines, a run on tickets, and Parnes breaking even.

When Kennedy bumped into Parnes again he took him to see Steele and the pair became his managers. They launched the effervescent cockney's career in ingenious style, making him play a debutantes' ball, which the press lapped up. Though Steele dreamt up his own name, Parnes insisted on renaming all his subsequent discoveries. Within a couple of years his 'Stable of Stars' included Marty Wilde (Reg Smith); Billy Fury (Ron Wycherly); Johnny Gentle (John Askew); Dicky Pride (Richard Knellar); Vince Eager (Roy Taylor) and Georgie Fame (Clive Powell). Only another cockney, the underrated guitarist Joe Brown, refused to accept his new chosen moniker: Elmer Twitch.

Despite their flamboyant image, the appeal of these pretty young men chiefly lay in their homely qualities. Colin MacInnes, author of the seminal novel *Absolute Beginners*, wrote of Steele: 'He is Pan, he is Puck, he is every nice young girl's boy, every kid's favourite older brother, every mother's cherished son.'

Yet Parnes could be brutal with his charges. In 1959, for example, he arranged a press conference for Vince Eager's nineteenth birthday. Complimenting him on his punctuality at rehearsals, he presented him with a new Triumph Herald. But after everyone had left, the man who had delivered the car drove it straight back to the showroom. Parnes explained that the whole thing was a stunt.

Likewise, Joe Brown worked for three years without a single night off. Sound familiar?

When Mrs Brown rang Parnes to complain that her son would collapse from exhaustion, Parnes sent two Harley Street specialists round to check she wasn't lying.

The young Svengali was also working the sponsorship and merchandising angles. A 1957 profile in the *Picture Post* noted a boom in Tommy Steele products. 'Flooding on to the commercial market are Tommy Steele shoes, Tommy Steele shirts, blouses, panties, skirts, ear-rings, bracelets, pullovers and sweaters. Before long, we are likely to see Tommy Steele lipsticks, face powders and foundation creams. Nightdresses may be coming soon – one can imagine the publicity campaign – Bedtime With Tommy Steele. The soft drinks industry has caught him up in their war because the soft drink which Tommy Steele drinks is going to be really important to their profit margins.'

This should ring bells.

All this success was based on a group of unrivalled contacts. A management contract with Parnes more or less guaranteed a recording deal, TV and radio exposure and a place in his touring shows, in which half a dozen acts would share the billing. Alongside A&R managers such as Hugh Mendl and Dick Rowe at Decca and Jack Baverstock at Philips, and songwriters like young Lionel Bart, chief among these contacts was Jack Good.

A former president of the Oxford University Dramatic Society and a stand-up comic, Good transformed the face of pop when he went to work for the BBC, and is the second key figure in the culture's history.

Teenagers in the early fifties weren't catered for by radio and television. Even if rock and roll was out there, you couldn't hear it – which makes a striking change from today, when you can't watch Titchmarsh doing some gardening without some drum and bass as background music.

Broadcasting was controlled by the BBC. Pop records were played on four radio programmes – *Housewives' Choice*, *Family Favourites*, *Down Your Way* and *Desert Island Discs* – for a grand total of about ten hours a week. There were, however, endless programmes of live music on which different singers and bands performed currently popular songs. The

Light Programme relented in 1955 and gave young listeners *Skiffle Club* on Saturday mornings, which soon mutated into *Easy Beat*. But even then not much changed because Musicians' Union rules meant that even these programmes had to rely heavily on the services of resident musicians.

Before the days in which hit records were turned into unique artefacts through expensive production work and the dominant projection of the artist's personality (Darius showed on *Popstars* how difficult it was to cover a track such as 'Baby One More Time'), it was songs, not singers, which were popular.

Every song was recorded by several singers. Record companies would invite publishers like Boosey & Hawkes to monthly meetings so that their A&R men could select suitable material for their artists. The publishers visited all the big four record companies – Decca, EMI, Philips and Pye – so there could often be three or four versions of the same song in the charts.

When a song was played on the radio, or whenever a piece of sheet music or a record was sold, the publishers received a royalty. Records were simply a way to boost sales of sheet music.

When the BBC introduced *Pick of the Pops* later in 1955, all that started slowly changing. The show played records selected at random from the Top 25 only. Then Radio Luxembourg began airing the complete Top 10 from across the Channel.

On television, meanwhile, there had been a show called *Hit Parade* in 1952 (revived in 1955) in which songs were performed by a team of residents, led by Petula Clark and Dennis Lotis, which was followed by *Off the Record*, featuring acts of the calibre of Alma Cogan and Max Bygraves, and Associated Rediffusion's *Cool for Cats*. This latter programme lasted fifteen minutes and involved discs being played and commented on by compère Kent Walton, sometimes with visual interpretations by The Dougie Squire Dancers. But revolution really took fire three years later when Jack Good landed a job as producer at the BBC of a new youth-oriented programme called *Six-Five Special*. Good had been sceptical about rock and roll until he'd seen *Rock around the Clock* at a cinema in Islington and explained his appointment by saying, 'I was the youngest person in the building in the time.'

Pete Murray introduced the first show on 16 February 1957 with the words: 'Welcome aboard *Six-Five Special*. We've got almost a hundred acts jumping here, some real cool characters to give us the gas, so just get on with it and have a ball.'

Jo Douglas then explained that for the benefit of older viewers: 'Well, I'm just a square, it seems, but for all the other squares with us, roughly translated what Pete Murray said was: "We've got some lively musicians and personalities mingling with us here, so just relax and catch the mood with us."'

Among those personalities – the first real rock and rollers to be seen on our screens – were exotic Yankees like Gene Vincent. But he wasn't half as exotic in real life as Jack Good imagined him to be, so when he appeared on the show Good took away his check jacket and dressed the confused Southerner in black leathers, hanging a medallion round his neck to create a twentieth-century Richard III. (Who, incidentally, went on to become a role model for the young Johnny Rotten.)

The American had suffered a motorcycle accident and wore leg irons, which gave him a limp. Good could see further dramatic possibilities. 'On the first show I made Gene walk down a staircase so the limp would be more obvious, but he came down the stairs too carefully. I had to run round the back of the set and yell at him: "Limp, you bugger!"'

Interestingly, in light of the look of the *Big Brother* household, Good made the action in the programme look as natural as possible. BBC bosses insisted on conventional scenery for the show, and didn't want teenagers dancing in the studio; Good mounted the scenery on castors, and wheeled it away when the cameras started rolling, ushering frenzied kids into shot, what the heck (it was all filmed live). And it didn't matter if a camera came into view, or if the set looked a bit wonky.

In the end, it all proved too much for Auntie, and Good decamped to the fledgling commercial channel ITV. There he started another show that was harder, faster, sexier, called *Oh Boy!* Its chief attraction became Cliff Richard.

It was at Jack Good's instigation that the former Harry Webb flipped his debut single, 'Schoolboy

Crush', and promoted the B-side instead, a real rocking number called 'Move It'. It hit number two in the charts in August 1958 and was subsequently acclaimed as the first real British rock and roll record.

Cliff became a regular performer on *Oh Boy!* His performances soon upset 'The Alley Cat' in the *New Musical Express*.

'This columnist has always high praise for the *Oh Boy!* television series,' he wrote. 'But producer Jack Good must be held responsible for permitting the most crude exhibitionism ever seen on British television by Cliff Richard last Saturday. His violent hip-swinging during an obvious attempt to copy Elvis Presley was revolting.'

Nonetheless, Cliff started alternating weekly on the show with Marty Wilde. Both sang their latest releases, plus all the big hits of the day. The nation – watching – soon took sides. It's hard to believe that it took another five decades for someone else to come up with a similar concept.

'Although we were quite good friends,' Cliff later recalled, 'a kind of Marty vs Cliff rivalry broke out. And he lost the battle . . . because of his management. They complained to Jack Good that I was being given all the best songs and all the best clothes.

'His manager said: 'If Marty doesn't get top billing, he's leaving.' That was a *big* mistake. Because Jack Good just said – 'Bye' . . . and I got the show to myself. And at the time, Marty was much, much better than I was. He was a great performer.'

By this time there were signs of social revolution elsewhere. In 1956 – the year of the Suez crisis – John Osborne's *Look Back in Anger* had opened at the Royal Court. Osborne was condemned as 'an intellectual Teddy boy'. With the plays of Arnold Wesker and novels of John Braine, the era of the 'angry young man' fully arrived. Indeed the working class became fashionable for the first time. Alan Sillitoe's *Saturday Night and Sunday Morning* was set in the terraces of Nottingham, Shelagh Delaney's *Taste of Honey* in the slums of Salford. The middle classes meanwhile were marching on Aldermaston for CND. And a show at the Whitechapel Gallery displayed blow-ups of advertisements and film stills, and a painting with a comic book and neon cinema sign. This was the beginning of British pop art.

Yet by 1960 the British pop industry was at something of a crossroads. Cliff had branched out into other forms of entertainment, appearing in his first film in 1959. *Serious Charge* was the story of a vicar wrongly accused of molesting a local gang leader (Cliff played the minor part of Curly Thompson) and carried an X certificate. Over the next four years, he picked tamer material. No one could really express revulsion at *Expresso Bongo*, *The Young Ones* or *Summer Holiday* – which might be the worst thing you could possibly say about them.

On Jack Good's advice, Cliff had shaved off his sideburns so he'd look less like a clone of Elvis. But the point about the first generation of British pop stars was that they only ever played at being rock and rollers. 'I used to be able to curl the lip too,' Cliff said years later. 'I can't do it so well these days. Back then, it felt quite normal. That was what rock and roll singers did.'

When Cliff received his first royalty cheque – for the princely sum of £60 – there weren't drugs around to blow it on, so he spent the lot on a telly for his family.

'Mr Parnes, Shillings and Pence's' 'Stable of Stars' mostly followed a similar career trajectory because Parnes thought of pop as a stepping stone to the worlds of film, panto and theatre. Tommy Steele, for example, turned himself into a family entertainer through flicks such as *The Duke Wore Jeans* (1958) and *Tommy the Toreador* (1959) before moving to the stage in the sixties (starring in something properly posh like Goldoni's *The Servant of Two Masters* at the Queen's Theatre in 1969).

It was also the beginning of the end for Parnes himself. He'd turned down Cliff after an audition and later failed twice to sign The Beatles. In 1960 he hired them as a backing band for Johnny Gentle on a tour of Scotland which proved a financial and musical disaster. Two years later he declined the opportunity to sign a deal to become their sole promoter.

In that decade, Parnes was eclipsed by a new generation of rock managers, such as The Beatles' Brian Epstein and Andrew Loog Oldham who looked after the Stones. In 1967 he announced that he'd outgrown the world of pop and, like Lionel Bart, who'd enjoyed stellar success with the musical *Oliver!*, would henceforth devote himself to the theatre (starting with a play about homosexuality in a Canadian prison).

In later years he managed the ice skater John Currie, before falling ill with meningitis and retiring. He died in 1989, having seen David Bowie imitate him in the role of Vendice Powers in a cock-shrivelling awful screen adaptation of *Absolute Beginners*.

In that book, first published in 1957, Colin MacInnes had already sounded the death knell of the teenage era.

'This teenage ball had had a real splendour in the days when the kids discovered that, for the first time since centuries of kingdom-come, they'd money, which hitherto had always been denied to us at the best time in life to use it, namely, when you're young and strong, and also before the newspapers and telly got hold of this teenage fable and prostituted it, as conscripts seem to do to everything they touch.'

If that suggests that pop culture was already corrupted – though I think in this country it was from the start and was really always in thrall to the wider world of showbiz entertainments – a corollary to that could be that everyone had it easy now. When he came to office in 1957, Harold Macmillan cut taxes and relaxed credit, further stoking the consumer boom. In July that year he made his famous remark that most British people had 'never had it so good'. There didn't seem to be much place in this new world for rock and roll.

Yet before his handsome win in the 1959 election,

'Supermac' abolished conscription, a move which had far-reaching effects for the future of British pop.

Without National Service, rock and roll groups became a real possibility. In the past, just as a band was getting somewhere, its members had to quit for two years. And even if that wasn't enough to ruin a group's prospects, there was no telling what time spent in the Forces might do to a young rebel's mind.

'I always thought it ruined Elvis,' Paul McCartney said years later of the King's military stint. 'We liked Elvis's freedom . . . but didn't like him with the short haircut in the army calling everyone "sir".'

In fact, the scene was set for the Swinging Sixties in 1960 itself, two years before The Beatles released a record, with the *Lady Chatterley's Lover* obscenity trial. The prosecution's case dissolved when counsel asked the jury if this was a book 'you would wish your wife or servants to read'. Then Richard Hoggart, a literary critic and defence witness, was asked whether the word 'fuck' gained anything by being printed as 'f***'. 'Yes,' he replied, 'it gains a dirty suggestiveness.'

Sex and class were back on the agenda.

Of course, by now the era of the old-style crooners was well and truly over, as one poor record cruelly testifies.

The Best of Dickie Valentine (Pulse, 1998) features some previously unissued concert recordings from the early sixties. In one show, Valentine, an accomplished comic and mimic as well as a crooner, runs through his Al Jolson, then has a pop at Elvis.

'You know, since I was last here I've been very fortunate in being able to travel pretty near all over the world,' he tells his well-heeled audience. 'And I've noticed throughout my travels that audiences, no matter where they are, whether it's in a nightclub, a concert hall, or a theatre . . . they all seem to have one thing in common; that is a taste for good music, whether it be jazz, classical or pop. And for that reason tonight I have chosen something which you will possibly think a little odd. But I would like to do this for two good reasons. The first being that I think it is very beautiful music, and second, and most important of all, this has what I consider to be one of the finest lyrics it has ever been my great pleasure to sing and I sincerely hope that you'll enjoy this.'

The pianist peels off a few notes, which everyone assumes will lead into a ballad. A pause. Then Valentine starts shouting out the words to 'Hound Dog', careering through two verses as the band behind him to do a pretty good impression of smashing up their instruments. It sounds pretty rock and roll, only Valentine really ain't the secret progenitor of that John Lydon.

Thirty seconds later they're finished. There are a couple of whistles from the crowd, and some clapping, but this quickly gives way to nervous laughter. Fortunately, Dickie reassures his fans that he hasn't come to eat them up, lapsing back into his marvellously urbane speaking voice to patronise Presley and his ilk: 'Thank you, thank you very much, music lovers.' Big laugh.

But Dickie's already begun to lose his cool and suddenly he sounds painfully embittered. 'Did you notice the words?' Cue more nervous laughter. 'Didn't you think the words were touching?' Then he puts on an Indian accent. 'They are the most beautiful words I have ever heard. It is making my heart go boom-tiddy-boom-tiddy-boom-tiddy-boom . . . goodness gracious me!' Back to Received Pronunciation: 'Those are beautiful words . . .

'Well, I see, looking around me here,' he continues, 'you all have a burning desire inside of you to hear the beautiful words of "Hound Dog". So now, I shall recite them for you.

'Could I have some dramatic music from you, please?' he asks the pianist, who strikes a solitary note. 'That's enough.

'You ain't nothing but a hound dog,' he begins to loud laughter. 'Crying all the time . . . You . . . you! Ain't nothing but a hound dog / Crying all the time. *That's just in case you didn't get the message first time.* You ain't . . . you ain't never, never, never, killed a rabbit . . . and you ain't . . . no friend . . . of mine . . . *Now, doesn't that move you?*'

Then it's back on with the show, with a nice joke about plans for a twist concert at the same venue the following week. 'The first prize will be two weeks' holiday in Port Elizabeth, and the second prize will be five weeks' holiday in Port Elizabeth.'

It's a horrible document. There's something truly excruciating about Valentine's patronising manner, partly because you suspect he's patronising part of the audience, partly because you know that he's pissing in the wind. It was already over for him and his kind, even if he did continue performing on the variety circuit up until his untimely death in a car crash in 1971.

Yet there were some survivors from this era. Johnnie Ray may have succumbed to liver failure in 1990, following years of alcoholism and a life in cabaret. But he lives on in the opening line of Dexys Midnight Runners' 'Come On Eileen', the biggest-selling single of 1982, which has itself become a classic.

And then there were people like Tony Bennett. He hit the top of the charts for the first and only time in this country with 'Stranger In Paradise' in 1955. In 2002 he duetted with Will Young at Her Majesty's Golden Jubilee Concert.

> *'I strongly disagree with the idea of artists having to stand up in public and be criticised by a panel of judges, it's too unkind'* – Hughie Green

Television grew up as a medium in the fifties and for most of the next five decades big programmes could depend on enormous audiences because there was precious little else to watch. I remember the birth of Channel 4 in 1982 and being thrilled that there would be 25 per cent more television on offer. Now we finally have cable in our house and there are *dozens* of stations – *endless* amounts of telly to watch. Of course, viewing habits have changed out of all recognition over the course of fifty years. People used to sit down in front of the television as if they had gone to the theatre. Father would summon the family as the set warmed up, and everyone would view the selected programme in silence. But soon enough the TV became a benign presence in the corner of the room, often with the sound down. It almost became like another member of the family. I certainly wouldn't let anyone who wasn't family or a pretty close friend watch me watching telly. The couch potato – that middle-aged creation – tends not to be a pretty sight.

In 1956 – the year of 'Rock Around The Clock' – ITV introduced a new programme taken from Radio Luxembourg called *Opportunity Knocks*. The contestants were amateur performers pitched in competition against each other. The talent could come from anywhere. One of the first contestants was Gladys Brocklehurst, a buxom Lancashire cotton-mill girl who would grab her husband Norman by the hair while she was singing and slap him. 'We do this for the fun of it,' she said. Other acts included a chef who cooked a complete veal dinner in under three minutes, a margarine sculptor and a dancer who kept tropical fish and danced the sailor's hornpipe. If Will and Gareth have their ancestors in the fifties, so does *Pop Idol*.

Opportunity Knocks was introduced by the avuncular Hughie Green, who is perhaps better known to people of my age as Paula Yates's secret father. At the end of each show, the studio audience evaluated each performance by clapping, and a 'clapometer' worked out who was that week's studio winner. But what mattered ('And I mean that most sincerely, friends,' said Green) were the votes of viewers at home, who wrote into the show with the name of their favourite act on a postcard. At the start of the following week's show, the winner was announced and given the chance to repeat his or her success. A winning contestant could return week after week, and at the end of each series, an all-winners show was put together.

Alas, Bonnie Langford was unable to appear for a second week when she won at the age of six because she had instead to go to a concert at her mother's dancing school, but over the course of its twenty-two-year history the show featured talent of the calibre of Bobby Crush, Lena Zavaroni, Les Dawson, Freddie Star and Little and Large. Su Pollard lost out to a singing dog when she tried her luck one year, but she made it as an actress in the end anyway. The show was revived with Bob Monkhouse in charge and then former winner Dawson between 1987 and 1990, when telephone voting replaced the postal system.

Opportunity Knocks was not a cruel show, and Green clearly cared for the acts. He was horrified in 1973 at the arrival of ATV's rival show *New Faces* on which a panel of expert judges were employed to help viewers make up their minds. These included record producer Mickie Most, who worked with The Animals, Donovan and Hot Chocolate in the course of his career; nightclub booking agent John Smith, 'possibly the least charismatic panellist in the history of television', according to one history of British TV; and journalist Clifford Davis, who once was slapped by a member of the audience when he gave ventriloquist Ken Graham nil for 'star quality'. He was christened Mr Nasty in the press. It all sounds terribly familiar. 'I strongly disagree with the idea of artists having to stand up in public and be criticised by a panel of judges, it's too unkind,' said Hughie Green. Equity, the actors' union, agreed, branding the panels too cruel.

Nonetheless, *New Faces* discovered Victoria Wood, Jim Davidson, Gary Wilmot and Lenny Henry, among others. Henry appeared at the age of sixteen in 1974, giving an impersonation of Frank Spencer with his back to the camera. When he turned round – 'Oooh, Betty!' – the audience howled at seeing a black man in the role. But not all the winners on the show went on to further greatness. Victoria Wood and the young Les Dennis were actually beaten in the All-Winners Final of 1974 by a teenage impressionist called Tony Maiden. He had already known fame as a child playing Little Albert, the stable boy, in *Black Beauty* on TV, and after his triumph enjoyed a two-year run on the West End stage. But he quickly faded from view thereafter and for the past decade has been reduced to making a living on the Benidorm cabaret circuit. It all feels a bit Hear'Say.

There were in fact singers among the winners on these shows. But none of them ever found the kind of fame that Will Young has already enjoyed. Tom

Waite won the *New Faces* All-Winners Final of 1973 but he 'didn't want to be a star', he said years later, and though he 'wanted to make an album I never got round to that'. Four years later laundry-van-driver turned charming folk singer Berni Flint won *Op Knocks* for a record twelve weeks in a row and subsequently had a Top 10 single. But he too hated the business of fame – 'Every time I performed, to me, it was a nightmare' – and was soon happily reduced to playing pubs and clubs. Impressionist Maxton G. Beesley, father of contemporary C-list celebrity Max Beesley, was a runner-up in the 1972 final of *Opportunity Knocks*, the Gareth Gates to Bobby Crush's Will Young. (The rival contestants they beat along the way included Steven Smith and his father, Jimmy, performing a medley of songs on drums and organ, and seventy-five-year-old Louisa Bearman from Bolton, reciting a poem about slum clearances.)

Following his relative success on the show, Beesley saw his fees for a gig quadruple overnight. 'That's the power that you've got being on television,' he said in an interview thirty years later. But he never escaped the north-east working men's clubs. 'That was very tough in the seventies ... if they liked you, they let you live.'

He refused to be bitter about the money made by his modern-day counterparts – 'Things like *Pop Idol* are a fantastic way of getting success so quickly,' he said, but added, 'What's lacking there is variety ... We should have a show like *Opportunity Knocks* back on the screen, with people of all ages and specialist acts, magicians, comedians. It seems to be very pop-oriented.' And he also sounded a nostalgic cry for the innocence of a bygone age. 'Everything's nailed down now. It's percentages. They've got managers and agents already in place. But God bless these kids for their tenacity.'

8

POP IDOL

'It was a move back to show business for show business's sake' – Mark Frith

Pop Idol could never be called a cool show. Unlike *Big Brother*, it was pitched squarely at the mainstream. Anyone my age who didn't have small children would surely be out and about on a Saturday night, not stuck in front of the box watching the creation of a star who would likely prove a clone of Cliff Richard. There shouldn't have been room for it in Tony Blair's Cool Britannia. The middle-aged judges gave the impression that they wouldn't know Eminem from a spotty youth on the street, while the studio set for the second half of the series looked incredibly old fashioned. Presenters Ant and Dec provided a reassuring presence, managing to be charming and funny without ever slipping into snideness.

'*Pop Idol* was quite full-on and quite glam and very, very glitzy in the way it was presented,' said Mark Frith from *Heat*. 'It takes a lot of guts to do that, because the current thinking is that we have to be ironic, we need to be a bit against that kind of thing. You know, it was a move back to show business for show business's sake.'

The show was dreamt up by Simon Fuller over dinner one night with Simon Cowell and developed with Nigel Lythgoe. *Pop Idol* would contain the best elements of *Popstars* – the reality element – and the best element of the other hot show of the moment, *Big Brother* – the audience participation. As a piece of TV it couldn't fail. And like *Popstars* and *Big Brother*, it would generate second-stream revenue, big time. People would pay to vote, and they'd pay to own a souvenir of the show at the end, like 'Pure And Simple'. But better than that, this time the project would be seen through to the end. 19 would manage the winner, and fix a deal with a record company, BMG, through Cowell, to release the winner's records. Because the audience had already voted, BMG knew they were on to a winner. Their market research, and advertising, had already been done for them. It would surely be like shooting fish in a barrel.

This time, Lythgoe would stay behind the scenes, but Cowell was dispatched to work on the show as a judge to make sure nothing cocked the whole scheme up. For back-up there was the benign figure of 'Dr' Neil Fox, the Capital Radio DJ, who would support the eventual winner on his show, and Nicki Chapman. The fourth member of the panel was Pete Waterman, who had known Cowell for years (he had produced Sinitta's 'So Macho', it turns out), but interestingly knew Fuller very little.

The show's hosts would be Anthony McPartlin and Declan Donnelly, young veterans of the showbiz industry who had started life working on the children's soap

Byker Grove. From there they had branched out into a short-lived career in pop as PJ & Duncan. The duo didn't write any of the songs for their first album and it sold half a million. They wrote half the songs for their next album and it sold half as well. They wrote all the songs for their third album and it bombed.

For most pop stars life would have ended there, at the age of twenty-one, but Ant and Dec moved back into television as presenters of the Saturday morning children's show *SM:TV Live*, turning it into the sort of programme that adults with fond memories of *Tiswas* could enjoy as much as its legions of younger viewers. Their gift was that they never disrespected the medium. Ant once said that, when they were presenting the programme, 'we never wanted to move to a niche slot at eleven at night so that we could be cleverer and bluer'. Dec was even more disarmingly candid and said that they wanted to emulate the success of Noel Edmonds, who had presented *Tiswas*'s tamer rival *Multi-Coloured Swap Shop*, (which weirdly I always preferred). They were perfect for *Pop Idol*.

What was a pop idol? None of the judges ever seemed too sure of the criteria during the series, but Cowell said he hoped the programme would produce a winner who 'actually means something . . . which is quite rare for a talent show like this. Most of the talent shows where one winner wins, whatever happens to them?'

Here was a good comparison with *Opportunity Knocks*. His interviewer pointed out that some winners of that competition like pianist Bobby Crush, went on to have successful careers? 'Yeah, that's a good point,' Cowell conceded. Then it all went a bit Monty Python. 'But how many years ago was that?' Peters and Lee? 'Peters and Lee, yeah.' Then Cowell himself made a list of other stars thrown up by talent shows, as if talking to himself. 'Jim Davidson, Lenny Henry, Marti Webb. Freddie Starr. Lena Zavaroni.' But did he think he had a Lena among the *Pop Idol* bunch? 'Well, if we only had a Lena, I'd give up now. I'm not looking for a Lena Zavaroni.'

In February, ten days before the show reached its climax, another interrogator asked the judge what sort of star he did have in mind when the whole thing had started. 'Well, if it was a boy, I expect we were looking for someone like David Cassidy and if it had been a girl, like Britney,' he said. By this stage there were only three boys left, so that meant someone from The Partridge Family – and that didn't sound terribly reassuring to me. Cowell also admitted that he already had a strong personal favourite among the remaining trio. 'Oh yes, of course,' he said, 'there's one I really want to win.'

The show was originally broadcast on Saturday and Sunday nights so that viewers didn't get bored with the process. The first people the contestants saw were a couple of producers from Thames TV, who weeded out those with truly nothing to offer the cameras. Then the judges were wheeled in to pick and choose the least hopeless from those left from the original 10,000. As with *Popstars*, there were lots of laughs to be had at the expense of those contestants whose opinion of their own abilities bore scant resemblance to reality. The girl who sang 'YMCA' as if she were at an aerobics class; the guy in sunglasses who recited Rick Astley's 'Never Gonna Give You Up' in a dull monotone; the bloke who threatened to thump Pete Waterman (that seemed more like it). Happy memories . . .

This in itself was cruelty TV par excellence, and the judges themselves were hilariously bitchy right from the off. There was one kid I thought pretty good. When the panel turned him down he broke down in tears and staggered out of the room. 'I thought he took that quite well,' deadpanned Cowell. The contestant, Ben 'Sexual' Sharman, as he styled himself, later wrote to the judge, complaining about his treatment: 'Thanks for putting me down on national TV.' It was too late already by then.

Cowell was quickly developing the profile of Nasty Simon, though Waterman could be equally hard on the hopefuls. They were a devastating double act. The poor kids couldn't hope to compete.

Waterman: 'You have the worst singing voice I have heard in my life.'

Cowell: 'Terrible, terrible, terrible . . . Some people, you know, we say take singing lessons . . .'

'But I've had singing lessons . . .'

Cowell: 'Well, sue the teacher!'

And with a meek OK and a thank-you and goodbye, the girl troops out.

Amid all the idiots, it was difficult to identify anyone

with real talent at this stage, but the panel knew it had something with Gareth Gates. He walked into the room with his spiky hair and grey suit looking like a pop star, but stammered badly when he tried to speak. The judges waited patiently, staring down at their notes. When the boy started singing, they all paid attention. Cowell raised his head in the languorous fashion of a reptile eyeing its prey. 'Stop,' he said suddenly, and told Gareth he was 'a hundred per cent' through to the next round. Waterman amazingly was almost lost for words. 'It's amazing, isn't it?' he babbled to the singer. 'You can struggle with words, but you don't struggle when the words come with melody.' Gareth could only nod in agreement.

Will Young was nowhere to be seen.

After a couple of further rounds, the contestants were whittled down to a hundred, then fifty. It was at this point that Waterman gave a clue as to what he was looking for in a pop idol, launching an astonishing (televised) attack on a girl who had the temerity to ask whether the contract she was about to sign with the programme-makers would let her write some songs if she won. 'Do you want to be a pop star or do you want to be a writer?' Waterman asked, as if he were talking to a ten-year-old.

'Both.'

'You can't . . . You can't . . . I'm giving you a reality sandwich here.'

'I could be the biggest songwriter in the world, for all you know.'

'I'll tell you what,' Waterman said, 'I'll put a million grand you ain't.'

People called Simon Cowell nasty, but he was a pussycat compared to this.

When we met, I asked Waterman about the incident. 'That girl was rude,' he said. 'Every real talented kid I've ever met does not ask that question. They take it for granted they will learn and then they will develop, and then they do it. The moment you get a question like that, you know they ain't talented. And if they *are* great songwriters, what the fuck are they doing in a *Pop Idol* competition in the first place? 'Cos everyone is looking for songwriters.

'All those kids who would have asked that question, I would have chucked them out of the show at that point because they obviously weren't talented.'

In the footage of that incident you can see someone raise their hand to chip in on the girl's side. That was Will Young, though no one called him to speak. He was still the darkest of horses, the very last person to be seen by the judges at the first audition stage, and only just picked by the judges for the final fifty. He made it through the next round too, but not without a run-in with Cowell. After his performance in the heat, singing The Doors' 'Light My Fire', Waterman was mildly enthusiastic ('you did wake me up and I thank you for that'), and 'Dr' Neil Fox and Nicki Chapman quite keen. Nasty Simon said it was 'distinctly average, I'm afraid'.

Will hit back – like some amphetamine-soaked crazy,

leaping over to throttle Cowell (not really) – politely begging to differ. 'I promise myself now I will NEVER compromise who I am,' he wrote at this time in his personal diary (later adapted for publication).

When the final fifty contestants were whittled down to ten, *Pop Idol* started broadcasting live on Saturday nights. It was at this point that the programme-makers invited our participation. The plan originally was that we would vote off whoever we liked least each week, but that made the voting more prone to rigging, and the process perhaps less palatable. Instead viewers rang in for their favourite performer, and the least popular person left at the end walked. 'People feel they shared the contestants' success,' said Mark Frith, 'there was a bond there.'

Yet unlike *Popstars* or *Big Brother*, *Pop Idol* didn't deal much in the business of reality TV in its second half. It would have been easy to perpetuate the comparison with *Popstars* through a docu-soap narrative that followed the contestants' lives offstage but *Pop Idol* ultimately turned against that. In its final weeks, there was footage of what the contestants had been up to in between shows, but the focus was firmly on their performances in front of the studio cameras each Saturday night. 'Simon Fuller wasn't interested in all that about styling, putting them in a house, making them live together,' Nicki Chapman told me. 'Living together: that doesn't happen in real life.' Simon Cowell was asked whether *Pop Idol* ruined pop by revealing how it was all done. 'I think *Popstars* did that more,' he replied. '*Popstars* was a bit like: "This is how the magician does his trick", because it showed the entire process. I think where *Pop Idol* differs is that it showed the process but, more importantly, because the public did make the decisions, it was making the public do what we do for a living.'

Henry's House made sure that none of the contestants had more time with the press than any of the others. The final week of *Pop Idol* saw the publicity machine go into hyperdrive, but before then there was a concerted attempt to keep the contestants out of the celebrity magazines and tabloids. 'From the beginning, when there were the thousand hopefuls, our priority was to make sure there was even and controlled publicity,' said one of Julian Henry's colleagues, Charlotte Hickson. 'When we came down to the last ten, all were given the same media quota and there were no national press interviews.'

All this suited Will, who sort of did have something to hide from the media. 'The show was about my singing and I didn't want to find myself in the papers because it would put me in the spotlight above the others – that wouldn't have been fair,' he said after the event. 'In the end, nothing appeared to take the viewers' minds off our singing abilities.' Thankfully.

But there were people paying attention to more than just that. A month before the end of the competition, Pepsi executives met at the company's British headquarters in Richmond, Surrey. Whoever the public chose to crown as their Pop Idol, the soft drinks company were already planning to hand a sponsorship deal worth £750,000 to Gareth.

'We started looking at Gareth from about ten weeks into the competition and realised that he was perfect for our brand of mainstream pop,' according to Karen Goffe, Pepsi's UK marketing manager. 'He also epitomises our "ask for more" corporate image. We were impressed by his fighting spirit and the fact that he had overcome a serious speech impediment to make his dream of stardom come true. He was always our first choice.' A million-pound deal between the spiky-haired wonder and gel and mousse manufacturers Wella followed too.

As the series progressed, it became clear to the contestants on the show that Simon Cowell too had long since recognised Gareth as his pop idol and wanted him to win. In the week before the final, Darius was speaking to one of the Henry's House team as he waited to be interviewed by Scottish Television on a link-up from London. The pair failed to realise that their mics were on and that their whispered conversation was being recorded. 'It makes me sick if it is stitched up or whatever; it makes me sick because Gareth is not the best contender for the competition,' the PR said. 'But he is the ch-ching factor.'

'But that's what they're always looking for,' Darius replied. 'This is out of anyone's control. And the problem is the men in black that really run the show. Do you know, playing the game is so hard when the rules get made up as you go along. You know what I wish?

That I was seventeen, I wish I was fucking naive and I wish I was blind and couldn't see any of this.'

The PR: 'And you just think it's all fantastic, yeah, but then you get stitched up.'

Darius: 'I know, I know, yeah. I feel so sorry for whoever wins this. It's a poisoned chalice.'

PR: 'It is, yeah. In my heart I want it to be Will.'

Darius: 'But do you know, in a way I don't want it to be Will – for him.'

PR: 'Because he's got too much integrity? And also it's not his style, is it?'

Darius: 'No, it's not. I think he'd hate himself for it.'

Then, after talking about Simon Fuller and Pete Waterman, the pair were finally interrupted when a production worker came to straighten Darius's mic. The singer looked a little panicked, while the publicist got up quickly and walked away from the mess.

No one from the *Pop Idol* camp would later comment on the incident – though good for Darius! But Waterman later did tell me, 'Simon had a favourite. Simon from the very first day that he saw Gareth made you quite aware who his favourite was. He helped him in any way he could.'

Here's the killer punch, however, for the notion that *Pop Idol* was in fact a stitch-up. 'I helped Will, in any way I could. So it was all counterbalanced,' Waterman revealed.

'Now the difference was Will didn't listen half the time. Gareth did exactly what he was told.'

Gareth Gates always seemed the most excited of all the contestants by those elements of the *Pop Idol* experience that did include the docu-soap stuff. When the cameras were filming the final four getting ready to go out for the night to a movie première, the bookies' young favourite made great play of opening his hotel window so that viewers at home could hear the screams of a gaggle of adolescents outside. When he was asked to model a pair of underpants featuring a roaring tiger's head for a photo shoot, he exclaimed: 'Ooh, the things you have to do to be a pop idol!' He was thrilled to be living this dream and almost acted as if he knew he'd won already.

In fact, the contest on *Pop Idol* developed into a struggle between Cowell and Waterman, as much as a battle between Gareth and Will. In Cowell's corner was someone who looked like the platonic ideal of a pop idol, and who was endlessly malleable to boot. Waterman, however, had spotted the guy with the real ability, and was later in a position to direct that talent. His problem was that Will could be a stubborn bugger.

For the first live show, the contestants could sing a song by their favourite pop idol. Jessica chose 'Papa Don't Preach' by Madonna (so-so . . .); Korben sang 'A Different Corner' by George Michael (hmmm . . .); Zoe picked 'I Will Always Love You' by Whitney (sweet Jesus); Laura chose 'She's Out Of My Life' by Wacko Jacko; Hayley decided on 'Made For Lovin' You' by Anastacia (good God); Aaron chose another George

Michael song, 'Jesus To A Child', and Rosie sang some tosh by Mariah Carey. Gareth sang 'Everything I Do' by Bryan Adams – for fuck's sake! I guess I would have been tempted to go for something like 'Holiday In Cambodia' by the Dead Kennedys if I were a contestant, which is in my range, and would stir things up. But I'm not now a pop idol. Will picked 'Until You Come Back To Me' by Aretha Franklin. Spot on! And that week, Will won the show, with 27.3 per cent of the vote (according to figures released after the series finished). Korben was last and left. Nicki Chapman blamed it on the funny hat he'd worn.

The themes of the next three weeks were Christmas songs; Burt Bacharach songs; and songs from movies. Adios, Jessica, Aaron and Laura! The contestants were free to make their own decisions about what they wanted to sing within the given guidelines each week, but by now the producers had become much more involved in the process. 'What we realised,' Waterman told me, 'was that if one of them sang a no-hoper, he was gone – the public would get rid of them. And to some extent it wasn't doing the show any good anyway.'

Waterman was allowed to give the contestants a real measure of advice because unlike Cowell or Chapman, or 'Dr' Neil Fox, he could have no direct stake in their future. 'That only went so far as I would pass an opinion,' he told me. 'I would not make a decision. But if they wanted it, I would help and guide them. Some did. Some didn't. But I was quite vitriolic when

I thought there were songs that I thought just weren't right.' This is what determined the course of *Pop Idol*, as Waterman tells it.

According to the record producer, the 'one show that really put the cat among the pigeons' was the Abba one halfway through the second half of the series. He wasn't involved in the decision to pick Abba songs because, as he insisted on telling me, he was suffering from shingles that week. 'And it was a disaster. Everybody knew it was a disaster. I know Abba's songs backwards. I've played them for a living and I know Bjorn and Benny. I walk into the rehearsals and there are the most glum faces in the world. I said to the directors, "What's wrong?", and they've said, "Pete, we're in the shit. This doesn't work." I go, "OK, what's the problem?" They've gone, "The songs just don't work." I've gone, "Oh, right, you've done Abba . . ."

'I had said to the contestants all along, "Please, lads, don't treat any of the songs you'll be singing as frippery – they are not." Right at the very beginning, I said, "Kids, understand, you will win this competition singing hits. You will not win this competition being clever. People will just think you're a smartarse. So try and understand the songs."

'We went into rehearsals and after two numbers I said, "Right, stop. Why the fuck did you do this? Why didn't you ring me, even though [again] I've got shingles? Why didn't you ring me and say, 'Should we do Abba?' I would have rung you back and said, 'No. It's far more complicated than you think it is.

The harmonics in these songs are crucial. Also, you can't suddenly take a part of a song out because you don't like it or you don't understand why it's there.'"'

Waterman didn't have time to change things around. The contestants went into the show that week woefully unprepared.

'Take Rosie Ribbons. "The Winner Takes It All" . . . she should have killed you. *"I don't want to talk/about leaving,"*' Waterman started to sing to me. 'No! They took all the beautiful chords away and went straight to the bleedin' chorus!

'Hold on! Whoah! You can't do that!

'You've got to set it up! It's not C, F and G . . . they're frigging *complicated* chords. Now, either play the chords, or say to the kid, "Hold on a minute, we can't work this out." You know, I've tried to play "The Winner Takes It All", and I had to ring Bjorn and Benny and say, "What the fucking hell is this chord? What is this?!"

'They said, "Well, yeah, it's not actually a chord, what it is, is . . ." And you go, "Shit, 'course it is."

"And what we did is, there's an octave there, and we put a flat and thirteenth there. So actually it's not a chord. We just made it up, it just sounded right."

"Right. Thank God for that. I've worked that out now."

'So when it comes to "The Winner Takes It All", you can throw music out the window because they've used harmonics to make it work. You take that out and suddenly the song's lost all its beauty.

'So, poor kid, she's exposed, she's dead. She's dead in the water. She can't sing this song, because there's no romance left . . . you've taken the magic out.'

The performance confirmed Waterman's worst fears. When Rosie Ribbons had sung before the judges at the first round of auditions, her performance had moved the record producer to tears (which is not a reaction I can imagine Simon Cowell ever experiencing). Now he was reduced to making her excuses, pointing out that the backing track she sang to 'had nothing to do with the emotion of the song'. Less perspicaciously, Foxy said the song didn't suit her voice, while Cowell complained about her dance moves. (Nicki was away.) Waterman had always said Rosie was going to be a superstar, but now she limped in last in the public's affections, with a measly 5.1 per cent of the vote.

The other contestants had struggled all the same. 'Who'd have thought Abba songs were so incredibly hard for me to sing?' Will said later. He thought he had the best of a bad bunch with 'The Name Of The Game', but in fact only Gareth, who sang 'One Of Us', really made it work. He romped home with 36.6 per cent of the vote, with Will a distant second on 25.2 per cent. Talking to Will on the programme that night, Pete fudged his comments, saying, 'It's a difficult one tonight. I don't want to be sitting here tonight, Will, because I thought you, all the way, pulled it off. I think it's tight tonight.'

It wasn't just the contestants who suffered. According to Waterman, as soon as the show finished that night, 'the TV station rang and said, "Pete's doing the music from now on. He's got to hear all the songs, make all the arrangements, because he's fucking spot on. And we've lost a kid tonight who we know he loved; he knows she should have gone farther. But these kids cannot have the knowledge of songs that someone like Pete Waterman has."

'Well, that's why you go to a record producer and songwriter in this business. It may sound uncomplicated but it ain't. That's why he gets paid millions of pounds.'

The following week, when the contestants had to do a big-band song, Will picked 'We Are In Love', a Harry Connick Jr favourite, against the advice of Waterman, who urged him to choose something by Sinatra. This was Waterman's real problem with Will. 'He was stupid,' he told me. 'If he'd sung Frank Sinatra, with the big band, Gareth wouldn't have stood anywhere near him.'

Fortunately for Will, Gareth made his own mistake. 'I laughed – I still laugh – when I heard Gareth sing "Mack The Knife". I fall about laughing! It's not even the tune. Simon and all them were going, "It was wonderful." I didn't say anything, because I didn't want to be rude. I didn't want to say that was fucking crap. But it was fucking crap. It wasn't even the frigging tune! I couldn't believe it! I was sitting there thinking not one fucking note of this is the tune.' That evening, Gareth won 25.4 per cent of the public vote, with Will on 24 per cent, but Darius took the opportunity (with a great performance of 'Let's Face The Music And Dance') to close the gap, pulling in 23.7 per cent.

The following week, Will again came second. The four remaining contestants sang songs that had previously hit the top spot in the charts. Gareth did Wham!'s 'Wake Me Up Before You Go-Go' and 'Unchained Melody', Will covered the Eurythmics' 'There Must Be An Angel' and 'Night Fever' by the Bee Gees, while Darius essayed 'It's Not Unusual' by Tom Jones and 'Whole Again' by Atomic Kitten. Zoe Birkett, the fourth remaining contestant, struggled with Jennifer Rush's 'The Power Of Love' and Whitney's 'I Wanna Dance With Somebody' and was duly booted off, much to Gareth's particular dismay. Darius was right on Will's heels, scoring 24.5 per cent, compared to his 27.9, and Gareth's 28.7.

That same evening, the three of them had a meeting with Cowell at which they heard demos of 'Evergreen' and 'Everything Is Possible'. The following morning they went into a studio to record the tracks, so that whoever won the show would quickly have a single ready for release. Will immediately felt that the songs were more suited to Gareth's voice than his. In fact, 'It almost felt like the songs had been chosen especially for Gareth.' It seemed that Cowell would have his way.

The next week changed everything. The judges picked the songs for the contestants to sing. Gareth did well with 'Yesterday' and Westlife's 'Flying Without

Wings', and Darius performed admirably with the Walker Brothers' 'Make It Easy on Yourself' and 'Dancing In The Moonlight', the Toploader version as much loved by Jamie Oliver. Will blew them both away.

He got Jackie Wilson's 'The Sweetest Feeling' and the Lawrence/Trenet number 'Beyond The Sea', as popularised by Bobby Darin. Waterman's hand was evident in both choices. When Will sang 'Beyond The Sea', Pete hailed the performance, saying, 'Although I learnt it at school in 1954, I just thought I would love to hear it . . . It's one of my favourites,' while he greeted the Wilson tune with 'Everyone north of Watford will be sitting and bouncing around their kitchens to that one'. There was an old Northern Soul fan speaking!

At the end of this penultimate show, Will had regained the lead in the competition, clocking up 39.8 per cent of the vote, with Gareth now trailing closely with 39.3 per cent. Darius scored just over 20 per cent, and went. His was one of the great *Pop Idol* stories. The country's court jester on *Popstars*, he had only sneaked into the final ten when 'Fat' Rik Waller, the bogeyman, withdrew after two rounds because of a sore throat. In fact, the narrative of the entire series read like a film script full of such incidents. In the end, two well-matched but different personalities – one with a serious speech impediment, to add further spice – were left. Great pop moments always seem to involve such friendly duels, and enjoy that dynamic.

Will destroyed Gareth in the final. It may have been that the public preferred his choice of 'Light My Fire' to Gareth's 'Unchained Melody', which the boys themselves picked to sing, but the easy point of comparison was between both performances of 'Evergreen' and 'Anything Is Possible'. Gareth did fine. You could easily believe that he was a member of Westlife up there on stage. But Will took things up another level, making the songs his own. And that was the end of *Pop Idol*.

Cue the jumping and screaming in our house.

It had seemed like the powers that be were conspiring to anoint Gareth, but in the end Will's natural ability shone through. In the end he won the final by a clear half-million votes. That made victory all the sweeter.

The first thing to say about Will's triumph is that though he came from behind in the end to win the series, and was never perceived as the public's favourite, he had led the field quite comfortably in the first four of *Pop Idol*'s ten final rounds. The only hiccup came with the Abba show. 'It was never as close as people thought it was,' Waterman said. 'Most weeks Will won by a long way – it was only towards the end that Gareth started to close the gap on Will and that was when Will started to become a little bit arrogant. I don't mean to you, the television viewer, but he did think he could sing anything. And to me he won it when he sung "The Sweetest Feeling". He pushed himself back out. That was my suggestion. He pushed himself back out in the lead and he wasn't going to get caught. I thought, "Fucking brilliant."'

9

THE SECRET OF SUCCESS

'Will Young's in The Guinness Book of Records, *for fuck's sake! But so what? So is a bloke who jumps off the Eiffel Tower and lands in a fucking teacup'* – Noel Gallagher

When Will Young walked offstage after winning *Pop Idol*, he was whisked into a meeting with Simon Fuller and Nicki Chapman to discuss the videos for his first two singles. Then it was on to ITV2 for a final interview with Kate Thornton and a load of pictures with the paparazzi before hitting the hotel for a party with his family. Five hours later he was on a plane to Cuba to start working, travelling with a new PA whom he barely knew. The next day, in Havana, they discussed his schedule for the next three months. Welcome to Planet Pop.

The death of Princess Margaret on the same Saturday as the final meant that Will didn't feature on the front of the following morning's papers. Even in 2002, the Royal Family were still the bigger celebrity draw. But the *Sunday People* provided an exception, finding room above its main headline of 'Anguish Could Finish Queen Mother' for a picture of the nation's new pop idol doctored so that he was wearing a crown. (The other strapline on the front page: 'Exclusive: My hell with the sex-mad school Miss, by virgin schoolboy'.) That week, *Heat* put Will on its cover, and for the next two as well.

With Will already out of the country, Simon Cowell took the opportunity to stick up for the loser. 'The final vote is irrelevant,' he was quoted as saying, 'Gareth is THE major pop star to have come out of the show.'

Other pop stars wasted no time in rubbishing the entire concept. Tjinder Singh from oh-so-hip Cornershop called the show 'pitiful ... the exact antithesis of everything we've worked towards ... a very frightening thing for music'. George Michael dismissed the phenomenon as nothing more than the product of 'interactive TV' – to which Simon Cowell cattily replied, 'It was only ten years ago he was sticking shuttlecocks down his shorts.' Ronan Keating, the former Boyzone singer, cheekily called the contestants 'glorified karaoke' acts.

In fairness to Ronan Keating (dread words), however, I shared his concern for the fate of the *Pop Idol* finalists. 'If I were them,' he said of Will and Gareth, 'I'd be wary. I think they are surrounded by people who are pushing the whole marketing campaign rather than nurturing the artist.'

The irony of *Pop Idol* was that it had been all about the talent – but the winner got to work with people who seemed to know only the art of marketing. William had shown that he was tough and could stick up for himself on the show, but this was the real world. So the country's new pop idol pronounced himself entirely happy with Fuller and the team at 19. 'I really do feel that we're on the same wavelength about my career,' he said. 'I think I'm going to be very happy. I trust them completely.' Cowell was quick to insist that Will would 'definitely have longevity' and could even crack America. 'I think he will move from the pop world to singing soul,' he added. 'It's all about having the right songwriters.' Nicki Chapman said, 'Gareth's a great pop star. I think Will is a cross-over artist.'

On 25 February, Will's debut, the double A-side of 'Evergreen' and 'Anything Is Possible', was released. In that week alone, it sold 1,108,659 copies. Some crossover.

For the record, the Top 10 on the Sunday read:

10. 'Shoulda Woulda Coulda' by Beverley Knight
9. 'You' by S Club 7
8. 'The World's Greatest' by R. Kelly
7. 'In Your Eyes' by Kylie Minogue
6. 'World Of Our Own' by Westlife
5. 'How You Remind Me' by Nickleback
4. 'Something' by Lasgo
3. 'Hero' by Enrique Iglesias
2. 'Whenever Wherever' by Shakira
1. Will Young!

The following Sunday, Will told the *News of the World* that he was gay. In fact, a press release went out to all the papers with the news to pre-empt the *Mail on Sunday* running some kind of story on Will's private life, which Henry's House had reason to believe they were preparing. Earlier in the week its sister paper had run a bitchy piece, laden with innuendo – Will would soon 'be whooping it up . . . at one of Elton John and his lover David Furnish's intimate little all-star soirees'.

The *News of the Screws*' editor, Rebekah Wade, rang Julian Henry herself to ask whether she might be able to help in some way. For her kindness, she got an exclusive interview in return, which presented the revelations in the most flattering manner possible. The interview kicked off with the assertion that Will has 'fame, fortune, adulation – and the courage of a lion'. The writer, showbiz editor Rav Singh, even thanked 'the great team at Henry's House'. This didn't mean that the Murdoch paper was entirely comfortable with the situation. Another '*Pop Idol* source' also told the paper, 'He is gay but is very discreet and not some gay rights fanatic. He doesn't try to preach to people about it.' But they needn't have worried. No one seemed outraged at the revelations.

In fact, the truth of Will's sexual orientation had long been common knowledge in the media and music industry. After the outing, the *Daily Star* claimed it had known all along but didn't publish anything because 'in 2002, the fact that a pop star is homosexual is hardly news'. Too right.

In the fifties, Larry Parnes' boys had to keep their

sexual orientation firmly under wraps. Now even management seemed quite easy about these things. 'I had a long conversation with the boss Simon Fuller last night,' Will told Rav Singh, 'and told him about my decision . . . He was totally relaxed and supportive and left it up to me to decide when, or if, I wanted to talk about it.' It might seem odd that Will should even seek Fuller's sanction, but the public appeared to share Nicki Chapman's view. 'We're dealing with an artist,' she told me. 'All that matters is talent.'

I thought it more likely that Will's poshness would count against him in the eyes of the public. His housemates at Exeter were called Pilky (Claire) and Milsy (Camilla), which illustrates the milieu in which he moved all right. Kate Thornton on *Pop Idol Extra* said she thought he was a bit of a bumbling Hugh Grant. Cowell preceded his infamous comment that Will was 'distinctly average' by saying: 'I had a vision of Sunday lunch and after Sunday lunch you say to your family, "I'm now going to sing a song for you."' Nothing wrong with any of that, and there have been countless middle-class rock stars, from Mick Jagger to the chap who sings with Radiohead (an Oxford boy). Yet whereas in the fifties public school accents received cap-doffing respect, in 2002 people like Damon Albarn from Blur talk mockney to ensure they're not sneered at. I guess that's one of rock and roll's victories. But Will didn't play that game. It was heartening that no one seemed to mind when it came to voting on *Pop Idol* or buying his records. Neither did Will's professed admiration for the novels of Iris Murdoch seem to count against him. This was that same tolerant Britain we had seen on *Big Brother*. We even tolerated Gareth.

Three weeks after Will had smashed sales records with 'Evergreen', it was Gareth's turn to top the charts. Even though he hadn't won the show, he had indeed also been signed by 19 Management and handed a deal with Cowell's subsidiary label at BMG. At seventeen years and eight months he became the youngest British male solo star to have a number one, beating a record held by Craig Douglas, who was eighteen and one month when he hit the top of the charts with 'Only Sixteen' in 1959. The song Gareth triumphed with was 'Unchained Melody', a chart-topper on four previous occasions, first in May 1955 for future DJ Jimmy Young, most recently in 1995 for Robson & Jerome, another of Simon Cowell's acts. (Paul McCartney's company MPL Communications publishes 'Unchained Melody', a nice earner for the former Beatle, incidentally.)

It seemed unfair that Gareth should be allowed to release a single so soon and Dec from the series stuck up for Will, saying that 'he was the *Pop Idol* winner and they should have held back Gareth's single for a bit. But instead Gareth is getting all the glory.' Soft Cell singer Marc Almond, who was busy walking the comeback trail in early 2002, also complained. 'Why do we have to put up with the *Pop Idol* losers and runners-up releasing records?' he moaned. 'It's all very

Saturday night karaoke. There's room for Will Young because he won the competition but the rest can fuck off.' Well, fair enough, in fact.

But if no one was quite sure what they had with Will, Gareth was plainly the perfect English pop star in the tradition of Larry Parnes' stable lads. When his single went to number one, he told the *Mirror*: 'I'm over the moon. It's something I've wanted all my life . . . It's awesome.' The rest of the report conjured the world of the *Picture Post*: 'Spiky-haired Gareth said: "I speak to my mum and dad every day and one of them travels down to London to see me at the weekends. At the moment I still haven't learnt how to use a washing machine. But I'm being looked after." . . . He intends to buy a flat in London soon and hopes to make the most of his pin-up status as he scouts around for a girlfriend. Gareth sipped a lemonade as we talked in a trendy London restaurant. In tight black top and jeans, he looked relaxed and flashed his trademark toothy grin often.'

Gareth said elsewhere: 'I am working with a fantastic management team and I know that whatever decisions they make, they will be really good for me.'

Interestingly, however, Gareth's single, though it ended up clocking a million too, didn't sell as fast or as much as Will's. And interestingly, the version of 'Unchained Melody' that Gareth released came with his own recordings of 'Evergreen' and 'Anything Is Possible' on the B-side (as an old music fan like me still insists on calling the other tracks on a CD). Will's had been better. Pete Waterman was emphatic on this. 'Gareth did not sell more records than Will,' he said to me, 'even though I agree with you that perhaps the song didn't suit Will as much. He still outsold him.'

Throughout *Pop Idol*, it turned out, viewers rewarded talent rather than the most likely looking (who was the contestant with the great human interest story too). This suggested that the audience for the show comprised people immune to the sour charms of contemporary manufactured pop, but nonetheless interested in pop music: fans, in fact, prepared to engage with the show through voting. People, in other words, like me. And if you were an old pop fan who felt left out of the world of Westlife and S Club and whoever else has come along since then, *Pop Idol* promised a way back into the music scene. It gave viewers a stake in the process of the charts again, at a time when the charts had grown meaningless to most people over the age of twelve.

Yet tied up in there, for me, was also a sense of nostalgia – nostalgia for that great pop moment when pop music takes over the world, a nostalgia encapsulated in my experience in Britpop. I loved the excitement, the newspaper coverage, the TV news reports, the sense that everyone was talking about this, whether loving it or hating it. It marked a great explosion of energy in the culture.

Of course, it's also preposterous to compare *Pop Idol* to Britpop. *Pop Idol* was a scheme dreamt up by a small clique of men to score big ratings and hits and make lots of money. Britpop involved the toil and sweat and genius of young lads wielding guitars. Once again, I call a Gallagher to the witness stand. 'I just want to know,' said Noel after the show, 'what were those fuckers hoping to achieve out of this? Did they really think they'd find the new Elvis? They've made a mockery of singing, of selling a million records. Will Young's in *The Guinness Book of Records*, for fuck's sake! But so what? So is a bloke who jumps off the Eiffel Tower and lands in a fucking teacup. Did he write "Strawberry Fields Forever"? No, so fuck off, you fuck.'

Britpop was also a true cultural phenomenon, drawing on the buzz around British fashion and the new flowering of the arts. There was Noel Gallagher and there was Julien Macdonald and there was Jude Law. And guess what? There they all were as guests of Blair's at No. 10. 'Britpop' was shorthand for the mood and aspirations of the nation. Unfortunately, however, those aspirations led in fact to *Pop Idol*.

So Britpop was really a lie – it looked to be about rock and roll in every elemental respect, but was about as threatening as a tea dance. Elvis may not have sung about bringing down the system, but in the context of white-sliced-loaf America in the fifties, his febrile conflation of white country music and black R&B carried its own political message (never mind those twitching hips). Rock has always been about rebellion, but 'Britpop' *said it better* than 'Britrock'. Oasis produced Oasis but Britpop turned them into vacant figureheads of rock's new celebrity aristocracy. Liam marrying Patsy Kensit – and then bunking up with an All Saint . . . Rock became consumed within the culture of All Saints and The Spice Girls, the tabloids and *Heat* magazine. From there *Big Brother* and *Popstars* and *Pop Idol* were in sight.

> *'Personally I wouldn't touch Gareth's cheesy stuffed crust!'* – Popbitch

What happened to the *Pop Idol* contestants? The dispiriting news was that as soon as Will and Gareth's singles had charted, they both joined the rest of the *Pop Idol* finalists for a tour of the country's arenas. I reviewed the show at Wembley Arena, travelling there on my own (again) by Tube, walking out into the freezing, rain-swept night, negotiating the traffic and filth around the venue, and taking my seat with 12,000 hyperventilating teenagers and their mums. I also had flu. It wasn't much fun.

Then – oops! – I did it again, heading up to Glasgow so I could meet Nicki Chapman at the SECC show: This time, fuelled by Irn Bru and the pick'n'mix counter by the bar and their E-numbers, the audience was even more enthusiastic. Earlier on the tour, in Sheffield, there had apparently been a new world record, when the screams from the crowd reached 112 decibels, the loudest ever recorded at a pop concert, like standing 40 feet away from a supersonic jet engine, when Gareth walked on stage. It was hard to believe it wasn't louder tonight when local boy Darius made his entrance, and indeed, when Gareth and then Will finished the first half, I had to put my fingers in my ears, like, I'm sure, Robert Muller of the *Picture Post* in 1954.

The really odd thing about the show was that after the first half, when the contestants took it in turns to sing songs from the TV series (starting with Korben doing some Wham! rubbish), the big band from week six of *Pop Idol* was wheeled on and the plucky ten started singing covers of fifties hits. This was to do with Simon Fuller's notion that big-band music was going to make a comeback, and that the pop idols might be the vehicle for this notion. It was bizarre, because none of the young children in the audience was familiar with this kind of material (where was the cheap skippy drumbeat?), and their parents' memories only stretched back to The Partridge Family, at best. Hell! Some were younger than me! But all the same, they seemed to love it. Funny, that.

The leader of the big band (The Big Blue) was a charming young man called Ben Castle, whom I met afterwards. (As it turned out, he is the son of *Record Breakers* icon Roy Castle, who made a couple of big-band albums himself in the very early sixties.) Castle explained that Simon Fuller had witnessed the revival of music from the eighties and the seventies and the sixties throughout his life, so the logical next step was back to the dawn of pop. It seemed odd that the country's youngest pop kids should be wooed with the sounds of the fifties, but to me also strangely satisfying. And I could see that Fuller might want to take Will down the Sinatra or even Bobby Darin road. And . . .

'That music has supposedly been so unfashionable for such a long time,' Castle said, 'but then Will says, "This next song is by Bobby Darin," and the crowd erupt. For the first couple of nights we were on the bandstand looking at each other, thinking, "This can't be happening!"'

(Later I tried to track down one of the ill-fated albums Roy Castle made – ill fated because the bottom fell out of the big-band market when The Beatles turned up – but to no avail. Yet a look at his obituary revealed that his big break came on *The Dickie Valentine Show* on TV a decade earlier. Neat.)

But for Will Young, at least, grown-ups were never going to be enticed by the charms of a singer who made his living entertaining their bairns. If Will was going to be a cross-over artist, playing aircraft hangars to pullulating pre-teens seemed a funny way of going about it. And yet there he was all over the pages of *Heat* and *Sneak* and *OK!* as well, and then came news that he was planning a duet with Gareth, covering 'The Long And Winding Road' by the Moptops. This was going to be the curtain-raiser to yet another tour in the autumn, featuring just Will and Gareth, plus Zoe, who had also now been signed by 19, as support. Will looked like being defined by the *Pop Idol* logo for ever after – like Hear'Say with *Popstars*. It made me feel like asking for 40p back from the people behind the show for the calls I'd made voting. They could afford it: it was estimated that this tour would net the two headliners £1.1 million each (£245,000 for performing; £850,000 from merchandising). Already, from their singles royalties, they were estimated to have earned at least £700,000. Finally, there were rumours that Will and Gareth would host *Pop Idol 2* in early 2003, which would earn the pair something like £600,000 each.

What went wrong? Perhaps Will had been chastened by his experience with Waterman on *Pop Idol*. He realised that he didn't know it all, and would have to entrust an element of decision-making to his management. But this seemed like going too far. He could have had more faith in the nature of the fans who had put him where he was in the first place, and he could have shown more respect for their sensitivities.

As for the rest of the pop idols: Korben had been the first to go on the show and went back to his job selling mobile phones after it, but then the *Pop Idol* tour took place. When I met Nicki Chapman backstage in Glasgow, she told me that Korben had been attracting interest from the West End. Jessica, meanwhile, had won the right to represent Britain in the Eurovision song contest (didn't win or anything, though). Hayley had done some presenting work on *This Morning*. Rosie had found a management deal and 'it's a good A&R man who's going to sign her', according to Nicki. Aaron hadn't stopped working, up in Newcastle, performing and 'doing openings and stuff'. And Laura had been offered a lucrative modelling contract and had been doing some presenting work, 'and she's done a sponsorship deal with a furniture company'.

'They've all done quite well out of it,' Chapman said.

I asked her whether any of them had gone rock and roll crazy on the road, and started chucking tellies out of windows like pop stars are supposed to do. 'No! No, thank God,' she replied. She made the point that most of them were level-headed types, that some of them had been to stage school, and all of them would make a serious fist at showbiz. 'They all harbour a dream of being a pop star, but in reality that dream doesn't always work, so you have to to be a realist in life. So you can follow a dream but, you know, follow a few.'

Darius, meanwhile, was signed by Mercury and cast as a smooth singer-songwriter. The press release announcing the deal conveniently forgot to mention his appearances on *Popstars*. Will had said he thought Darius was the most complicated of the final ten contestants. 'I can't help but admire his drive,' he noted later, 'but I also can't help but find that a bit daunting.' And then Darius did have a Number One hit.

'Fat' Rik Waller signed a deal worth a reported £400,000 with EMI, while Sarah Whatmore, who was eliminated at the final fifty stage, was signed by

19, and Fuller said she was 'going to be the coolest girl in Britain very soon'. Hurrah!

There's even a happy postscript to the *Popstars* story. The finalists who didn't win turned themselves into their own group, called Liberty X, and slowly transformed themselves into a glammy garage act. In May 2002 they scored a number-one hit with their single 'Just A Little'. They were said to be 'over the moon'. And Kym Marsh that same month signed a six-album deal with Universal Island which, she told *OK!*, would let her get involved in the writing side of things. So perhaps my ears were deceiving me all along, and she can sing.

Pop Idol also turned the judges into celebrities. Nicki Chapman already had a public profile from *Popstars* and 'Dr' Neil Fox was a well-known DJ. But without *Pop Idol*, you can bet they wouldn't have found themselves hired to star in a Pizza Hut ad. News of this venture was greeted with much hilarity on Popbitch: 'Remind me not to order the Will Young meat feast . . .'; 'Personally I wouldn't touch Gareth's cheesy stuffed crust!' In the end it was a pretty tame affair, with the four arguing over which quarter of the new Pizza Hut Quad pizza they'd like. Nicki mediated and made sure everyone got what they wanted. 'No arguments, just loveliness.' But Simon, of course, had the final word: 'I still think my quad is far superior to yours.'

Cowell went on from *Pop Idol* to star in the States as a judge on *American Idol – Search for a Superstar*. 19

sold the show there after its success in Britain. It was inevitable that the producers there should want a slice of Mr Nasty – Brits are always typecast as villains in Hollywood movies, after all. 'Simon Cowell's kind of brutal honesty is not something we have experienced before,' said a Fox TV spokesman. 'People are going to take to Simon; to love him and to hate him at the same time.'

The show was launched in the States in June 2002. On the first episodes, a contestant called him an ass and fellow judge and eighties star Paula Abdul asked, 'Why do you have to be so rude?'

But Cowell also continued his career as a successful A&R man, working with Will and Gareth, who had both signed to his S Records, among others. 'Right now,' Ajax Scott from *Music Week* said to me when I met him not long after Gareth had gone to number one with 'Unchained Melody', 'Simon Cowell could release a record featuring your niece playing the recorder and BMG would get behind that. They would mobilise the machinery because his track record means he has that kind of leverage.'

19 held all *Pop Idol* artists' recording rights, but had agreed to license them to S in every territory. So Simon Cowell would make squillions from sales of Will and Gareth's records, an estimated £2 million from his participation in *American Idol*, and squillions more once the winner there put out a record with him.

Despite all this, Cowell made the point that *Pop Idol* wasn't just good for him, it was good for the industry as a whole. 'Whatever profits are generated by *Pop Idol* for BMG don't go into a *Pop Idol* fund,' he said. 'They provide more marketing money, promotional money and more A&R money.' He claimed as well that *Pop Idol* has encouraged school leavers to seek a career working in the music industry.

In fact, *Pop Idol* did do three brilliant things for the industry.

One: it found new talent, at a time when the industry had no idea where it was coming from.

Two: it sold lots and lots of records. As Pete Waterman said to me, with only slight exaggeration, 'By Christmas *Pop Idol* will have sold seventeen million records; Noel Gallagher will have sold 120,000. There is a fucking huge gap here!'

Three: it made people like me buy pop singles again. It made me interested in the charts again because I wanted to see who Will was up there against.

But *Pop Idol* couldn't count on securing that interest once the show was finished on TV, once Will and Gareth had faded from our screens. 'Remember, there is no guarantee in anything,' Cowell said. 'I think we have given ourselves an amazing head start but it ultimately comes down to the artist and the record. We feel confident this is just the beginning.'

'No one can tell whether [*Pop Idol*] is a blip, or the future,' he said elsewhere. 'The only way we can know is by keeping in touch with the public. And all you can do is do whatever you need to do to keep ahead of the competition, which *Pop Idol* has done.'

That was the challenge to everyone in the industry.

Simon Fuller continued to keep his head down in the immediate aftermath of *Pop Idol*, but it was fantastic business for him as well. Income from the phone voting alone generated an estimated £2.5 million. BT took 36 per cent of that, with Thames TV, the ITV network and 19TV divvying up the rest. Then Fuller jointly owned the UK and overseas television rights to *Pop Idol*, together with Thames, the UK television production subsidiary of RTL, a German television group now owned by Bertelsmann (like BMG). Each time the *Pop Idol* format was sold abroad, Fuller received royalties. And in every territory, he would also have an option to manage the winners' careers.

In Britain, the final ten on *Pop Idol* had signed contracts with 19 Management which reports said prevented them releasing a record at the same time as the series winner for three months after the end of the show. 19 had an option for a further three years on their future earnings, during which time it could demand 20 per cent of their music earnings. It then had a further option for fifteen years, claiming 20 per cent for the first nine and 10 per cent in the final six.

Popstars had been sold all over the world. I was in India in the early months of 2002 and watching MTV when a trailer for their version of their series kicked in. A show like this would have been unthinkable in that conservative country a decade ago. And *Popstars* also returned to UK screens in late 2002 in a tinkered version called *Pop Rivals*. Very similar programmes flourished too. In France *Star Academy* was a huge hit, while in Spain a record 15 million viewers watched the live final of *Operation Victory*. In early July 2002, the BBC announced plans for *Fame Academy*, billing the show as a mixture of *Big Brother*, *Pop Idol* and *Fame*, launching the series in the autumn against *Pop Rivals*.

Even just as a piece of TV, *Pop Idol* was an even bigger success than its progenitor. It won the top prize at the Montreux Golden Rose television festival in 2002, beating 296 programmes from around the world. Peter Bennett-Jones, the chairman of the jury, said, '*Pop Idol* was the clear winner of the Golden Rose. It combined a traditional talent show with the contemporary appeal of innovative audience participation through telephone voting. It not only unearthed genuine new talent, but was also the perfect family entertainment series.' Well, yes, mate, but that's barely scratching the surface.

Sure enough, other formats soon felt the hurricane of Fuller's creation. Cilla Black's *Blind Date*, a Saturday night fixture in the schedules for eighteen years, was revamped at the cost of an estimated £1 million to include ideas pinched from the series (more behind-the-scenes footage; a spin-off show on ITV2 carrying grittier details, and so on). An ITV1 source told the *Sun*: '*Pop Idol* was such a phenomenon that every entertainment producer is looking at taking up some of its most successful elements.' The BBC adopted a more highbrow approach, and ran a national IQ quiz involving elements of viewer participation.

Given this, Fuller had reason to be bullish about the launch of *Pop Idol* in America, particularly following the success of other British programmes such as *Millionaire* and *The Weakest Link* there. The publicity for *American Idol* billed the original as 'the biggest thing to hit Great Britain since the Beatles'.

This was actually brave of Fuller, given that in April 2002, two months before his show went on air in the States, there were no British singles in the US Top 100 for the first time in forty years. Here was a telling mark of the decline of the British industry. But of course, Fuller was launching a TV programme as well as ultimately an artist. And in any case he said Americans had never understood pop music, and that this would be the show to make them see the error of their ways. The programme became the hit of the season.

His ambitions didn't stop there. In an interview with *The Times* two months after *Pop Idol* reached its climax, he revealed that he had been working on a new concept. *The Greatest Show on Earth* would be a global talent show simultaneously broadcast in over fifty countries around the world, so that one TV appearance would place an act in front of 400 million people.

Even more mind-blowing was his idea of developing a virtual star, a computer-generated singer who would look like an alien and be able to speak any language on Earth. 'I think when virtual reality really kicks in,' he told the interviewer, 'it will be pretty scary and will probably culminate in the end of the planet.

But from an entertainment perspective it will really throw up some amazing opportunities.'

10

PETE WATERMAN IS GOD AKA WORDS I THOUGHT I WOULD NEVER WRITE

'Whatever happened to the kids? You used to be able to depend on them to stir things up?'
– Sunday Times

So where did my nostalgia for the great pop moment reside, if not in the early celebrity culture of Britpop? (Funnily enough, in 2000 Damon Albarn had launched a virtual band himself, Gorillaz, which proved a far bigger international success than Blur.) It never quite happened with acid house or Madchester for a variety of reasons, at least for me, and it sure as hell didn't happen in my indie years, or at Live Aid. Perhaps the answer lay in the dawn of the eighties, when the tabs and the new pop press were filled with screaming youth. But the industry sales figures for those years don't bear out that diagnosis, and what was Adam if not the man who set pop stars firmly back on the showbiz track after the distractions of the sixties and punk? Tommy Steele was no different to Gareth Gates, was he? Perhaps I had never known a pop cultural explosion worthy of the name. All my life, I'd been living a lie, trying to conjure some sense of such a moment, and my attraction to *Pop Idol* was simply wishful thinking. *Pop Idol* provided a simulacrum of such an event but nothing more. So perhaps my interest had been of the post-modern sort. *Pop Idol* did mark a return to show business for show business's sake and it wasn't cool. So when I told people I was hooked on this smorgasbord of light entertainment, most assumed that I was watching with a sense of irony.

My generation had apparently reconciled itself to the charms of mass entertainment – even people like me with years spent howling in the wind as indie kids – by becoming ironic consumers. It was perfectly OK to like crap TV because we were watching it with a knowing grin. It was OK to say you liked early SAW because of its very naffness – now you thought it was always meant to be kitsch, rather than merely rubbish. Of course, this was really a retreat into infantilism, which is why the most popular club night in Britain in 2002 was not Cream or another house superclub but School Disco, at which thousands of people in their twenties and thirties put on their blazers and gym slips to dance to the fabulous hits of the eighties. Television and the pop industry inevitably started churning out product with a degree of irony built into the formula: Graham Norton's TV chat show, or those *Top 10* or *I Love The . . .* programmes; Robbie Williams singing Frank Sinatra; even hip acts like Fischerspooner, who winked at past fashions in their sound and imagery. It seemed that my contemporaries had thrown in the towel when faced with the insidious charms of modern entertainments; there wasn't any fight – there wasn't any rock and roll. Or if they hadn't, they thought they could get the contest called void by treating the whole thing as little more than a laugh.

Irony's handmaiden is camp, and there was something quite camp about *Pop Idol*. It was there in the sets and the nature of the presentation and principally in the character of Simon Cowell, the great pantomime dame, though his fellow judges weren't far behind him in these stakes.

I concede: there's no point denying there was an element of pleasure in that. But was that really why I liked *Pop Idol* after all? As an ironic mockery of pop culture?

In 1975, the *Sunday Times* asked: 'Whatever happened to the kids? Mods, rockers, beatniks, greasers, flower-children, hippies – you could depend on them to stir things up.' Well, within twelve months they had punk. But perhaps that was youth culture's last real stand – a call to get real, and I missed it. We can't escape our synthetic future.

> *'I don't have to sell my soul ...' – 'I Wanna Be Adored'*

About all these things I worry too much. Pop – rock, rockabilly, techno, hip hop, country, even skiffle, I'm guessing – is all about losing yourself in a moment. At its heart is the fact that it pulls off a fantastic contradiction: pop functions through the mass media, but it talks to you alone, as an individual. My authentic rock moment wasn't seeing other kids wearing Butthole T-shirts, it was listening in my childhood bedroom to *Locust Abortion Technician* (the band's fifth and arguably finest album, though others prefer the subsequent *Hairway To Steven*). It wasn't the three-hour round trip on my own to see Spacemen 3 in a toilet in Aylesbury; it was losing myself in their blistering version of 'Revolution' (however silly the lyrics). It was pressing my head against the speaker stacks at the Oxford Poly to really feel the noise. It wasn't wanting a pair of baggy troos or a T-shirt like Ian Brown's; it was the feeling I got listening to 'I Wanna Be Adored'. It wasn't watching Liam's swagger, it was the swagger playing 'Live Forever' gave me. But of course it was all the other stuff! Because otherwise I'm perilously close to breaking down and sobbingly confessing that I've always secretly been a fan of Pete Waterman's records.

> *'You have to be a little bit careful not to take the chicken out of the chicken soup. Music is always the chicken'* – Pete Waterman

Throughout his career, Pete Waterman has never been interested in videos or marketing or sales pitches or new formats. 'DVD? I don't give a fuck about DVD,' the most successful producer in British pop history said to me. 'Play me a good tune.' According to Waterman, the problem with the industry today is that the men in charge at every level have forgotten what it is that makes music such a marketable product. 'I say to the radio stations,' said Waterman, '"Don't you think you should just play a few hits?" But everything now has to be researched. They don't feel it. They don't put a record on and go, "Fucking hell, I love that. I don't give a shit that it's Engelbert Humperdinck, I'll play it." They say, "It doesn't fit our demographic."

'Fuck demographics. How can you research whether you love or hate a record? Does it give me goose bumps? There's my research. "It gives me goose bumps; we'll put it out."'

Waterman had some ropy years after Kylie went her own way and his later acrimonious split with Stock and Aitken. But in the nineties he roared back with Steps, and produced Westlife's single 'I Have A Dream' (for Simon Cowell), which was number one in the pop charts in Britain at the Millennium.

'I'm still selling five or six million records a year,' Waterman continued, 'because I don't believe in research. I believe in what my gut tells me. A good song is a good song and I don't know care whether it's Eminem or Nickleback or whoever. Pop music is exceptionally researched, but even more within the genre of the rock sector. But at the end of the day it's all down to whether you like the song. If you write a hit, people will give you lots of money. If you tell them it's a hit and they don't like it, they don't buy it. It's as simple as that.'

As he says: 'You have to be a little bit careful not to take the chicken out of the chicken soup. Music is always the chicken.'

I mentioned to Waterman the idea that pop acts can be treated like soft drink brands. 'I've heard that speech before,' he said. 'It was from a manager called Tom Watkins.' Watkins used to manage Bros and East 17. 'He was a fucking idiot. And if the people think they can brand S Club 7 like a can of Coke, they're wrong. If they think they can sell music as brands, they're wrong. Yes, if you are Oasis you become a brand; if you are S Club 7 you are not a brand, you are as good as your next song. If the people involved in *Pop Idol* don't know that, they have a problem with Gareth and Will, because they're as good as their next record. 'Cos you don't need Gareth's record if you're thirsty tomorrow morning. So that's an interesting conversation and it may be their philosophy. I don't know. But if that is their philosophy they're stupid.'

Everyone likes a good song, that's the truth of this matter. The real lie in this book is that throughout the eighties I was a huge fan of Prince, as well as those indie whelks, not because I identified with him particularly but because I loved his records. Today, there are some brilliant pop acts, though they mainly operate out of America. Destiny's Child are a fantastic group – it's not just owing to the fact that Beyoncé looks so Beyoncé – and I *lurve* Missy Elliott. As for acts from these shores, I really don't try to buy into the culture of So Solid Crew, but '21 Seconds' was one of the best singles I'd heard in years. I even – here it comes – liked 'Pure And Simple', and I've got a soft spot for some of the candyfloss being spun by Fuller's camp, like 'Wannabe', or that S Club

Juniors disc. But it's like what John Squire said about amplified sound. It's all music.

The creative wellspring in American r'n'b and hip hop often lies behind the studio desk, not in the vocal booth. That's where you'll see Dr Dre working (the producer of NWA's 'Express Yourself' and early Eminem) or Timbaland or Missy Elliott (whose success is rooted in her reputation as a producer). When it comes to dodgy British teen pop, the talent is usually the songwriter.

A host of eighties pop stars followed their first flush of success by moving behind the scenes and into songwriting. Andy McCluskey of Orchestral Manoeuvres In The Dark provided songs for Atomic Kitten; Alison Clarkson, aka Betty Boo, wrote some of The Tweenies' biggest hits and fashioned 'Pure and Simple' for Hear'Say; Cathy Dennis wrote songs such as 'Evergreen' for Westlife – as covered by Will Young – and 'Can't Get You Out Of My Head', in partnership with Rob Davis, former guitarist with seventies glam rockers Mud.

Rick Astley, who had been terrified by his early dose of fame with SAW, returned to the fray writing for others. One of his clients was Lauren Waterworth, a fifteen-year old schoolgirl discovered and recorded by Pete Waterman in 2002.

While someone like Will would die of embarrassment at the thought of speaking out of turn about the industry, some of these veterans have talked candidly. 'Pop artists like Kylie Minogue need the killer songs every year,' said Rob Davis. 'They have to do interviews all day. It's really time consuming, and writing and production is a full-time job. They can't just go away and spend ages making an album.' Alison Clarkson was less keen on the state of play, complaining about her clients' lack of genuine pop acumen. 'If you asked them about music, they wouldn't have a scooby-doo,' she said. *Popstars* came in for particular criticism. '*Popstars* was the whole thing I completely loathe in pop music. I don't like the idea of people being auditioned to be in a pop band. They may as well be working on a cruise liner. Pop music will not evolve if it carries on like this.

'I think *Popstars* exposed how a pop group is made. It should put an end to it completely. Even if "Pure And Simple" was a successful record, I'm not that passionate about it. I'm more passionate that the programme itself might have changed people's view about pop.'

Other stars of the eighties arguably fared less well. In the spring of 2002, a roadshow featuring relics of the New Romantic era, including Howard Jones and members of Spandau Ballet, toured Britain's arena venues. There were two ironies here: this was the generation that spearheaded the rise of style over content in pop culture, but now they'd run out of ideas. Yet that didn't matter, because their audience had grown fond of nostalgia and irony. Outside the SECC in Glasgow after the *Pop Idol* show, there was a screen with news of coming attractions. Hear'Say had cancelled their autumn date; instead you could see the

Here and Now tour. It was better to be a shit old pop group than a shit new pop group.

Adam Ant was supposed to be on that tour but pulled out after his arrest for possession of a firearm in early 2002 and subsequent hospitalisation for the sake of his own health. When the hits dried up and the Ants split, Adam had gone to Hollywood to pursue a career in the movies and did weird things like date Heather Graham. When that went belly up, he tried his hand at pop again, but didn't have the mojo to make it work for him again and couldn't escape his old image. 'It is not nice when people come up saying: "Didn't you used to be Adam Ant?"' he said shortly before his untimely arrest. 'I do have a pulse, you know.'

By the early nineties, Kylie Minogue 'wasn't primarily interested in making pop records for her public, but for herself instead', according to Pete Waterman.

Against his advice, she masqueraded as a bit of a tart for the video to 'Word Is Out'. It peaked at number 16 in September 1991 – her first single to fail to reach the Top 10. Not long after that, the pop princess signed to the hip dance label Deconstruction, and tried to reinvent herself yet further. In 1995 she hinted at a yet more deviant side by making a single with Nick Cave. By 1997 she had developed into a fully-fledged indie chick, and started collaborating with the Manic Street Preachers. Not surprisingly (not in my book, anyway), 'Some Kind of Bliss', her single written by James Dean Bradfield, only made it to number 22 on release in September 1997.

But in 2002, Kylie is one of the country's few bona fide pop idols (she's an adopted national treasure). Perhaps she had to go through indie ignominy to realise that the energy in pop culture these days genuinely lies in pop not rock. And here she was, revealed as a disco-dance sex kitten. And here she was, posing on the cover of *GQ* magazine in a parody of that Athena poster of a tennis player pulling up her skirt to reveal her bum. And here she was on the cover of *The Face*, as their star of the year. And here she was, in the video to 'Spinning Around', making further play of her greatest asset.

But of course her success was not reliant on her butt or her willingness to play the pop pixie again with the tabs (until the *Mirror* turned on her) and *Heat*. It was due to the fact that she had some of the best writers in the business working for her. Kylie started diversifying into her own range of underwear in 2002, but the real secret of that brand's success would always lie in how good her records sounded.

In fact, she had gone shopping herself, for the finest songwriters in the business again. Ten years after 'Word Is Out' fell flat, she had her huge number-one hit with 'Can't Get You Out Of My Head'.

Despite what Noel Gallagher said, it didn't matter that Will Young, like Kylie, wasn't a songwriter. Of course, the fact that he was just a voice – a voice to hire – militated against everything I'd learnt about rock and roll. Rock likes to think of itself as a kind of art, and its artists as Romantics, who wait for the muse to strike them before vouchsaving their creations to the world. Check out that constipated look on Noel's face when he's singing his songs on stage.

But I think it's fair to point out that, for all his achievements, like Will, Noel hasn't written a 'Strawberry Fields' either. It might mean drawing a line under fifty years of rock history, but I don't think there's anything wrong with facing up to the fact that a great interpreter of songs is the artistic equal of someone who's also written the stuff himself. Elvis's irony was that he started rock and roll – but has never really been loved by the rock cognoscenti (though there are signs of that changing now). In fact, ever since Dylan and The Beatles gave the world the idea that anyone can pen a masterpiece, a view endorsed by punk, it's arguable that the quality of songwriting in pop has been in sorry decline.

> *'I think people like to be entertained. And they know talent'* – *Nicki Chapman*

The reason *Pop Idol* worked was that the music was so great. I watched the first half laughing at the aspirant contestants, but the reason I got hooked was that the kids singing those old faithful hits in the studio each Saturday night were so bloody good. I didn't laugh at the final ten – very much – or view them as kitsch performers. I wanted to hear Will sing 'The Sweetest Feeling', even Gareth crooning 'One Of Us', or even – God help me – Darius singing 'Let's Face The Music

And Dance'. In fact, the reason I voted – and the reason why everyone voted, surely – was to make sure of hearing my favourite contestant again the following week. That was why we voted *for* contestants, rather than against them. That was how the competition worked. That was why the element of audience participation worked.

I asked Nicki Chapman why *Pop Idol* worked. 'It's all that thing of empowerment, isn't it?' she said. 'And there's that side of people wanting to have their say. What is it about our characters now that we do want a say in people's futures?' She paused to reflect, staring into the middle distance. 'Odd.' Then she tucked back into her lasagne. I waffled on about the psychology of *Pop Idol* and *Big Brother*. Nicki wasn't really listening. Then she snapped to, and hit on something else. 'I think people like to be entertained,' she said. 'And they know talent.'

What if Pete Waterman had been in charge of *Pop Idol*? 'I wouldn't have picked those songs,' he said, meaning 'Evergreen' and 'Anything Is Possible'. 'I wouldn't have picked that end.' As it was, his influence was limited. And yet . . .

'Simon Cowell and Simon Fuller were always going to call the master shots,' he continued. 'But in a way Simon [Cowell] didn't get what he thought he would because in the end the public did vote against him. And I think that's great.'

Pete Waterman had never had any stake in the *Pop Idol* contestants' futures but he left the show with his reputation considerably enhanced. 'I couldn't have a worse press if I had spent every night killing grandmothers,' he once said. Now people held him up as some kind of guru. At least, I did.

Then there was promising news. Gareth had inevitably started work on his debut album with Jorgen Elofsson, Per Magnusson and David Krueger, who had previously written for Westlife. But Will was working . . . not with Pete Waterman, but with Cathy Dennis and Burt Bacharach himself. It could have been far, far worse.

11

THE REAL REASON I LOVED POP IDOL

'This is all a peculiarly thin and pallid form of dissipation' – Richard Hoggart

Here's the real reason *Pop Idol* worked. There's a brilliant story about The Beatles going to visit the Maharishi in Rishikesh in India, which is somewhere I've been. Beautiful place. Now, after a number of days spent meditating and writing songs and, frankly, dicking about, in the company of Mia Farrow and Mike Love (who was always made out to be the least cool member of The Beach Boys – go figure), the Maharishi says he's going for a chopper ride over the Ganges. One person is allowed to go with him and, after a bit of umming and ahhing, John wangles it. Why were you so keen to go? Paul asked him later. 'To tell you the truth,' John replied, 'I thought he might slip me the answer!'

It was a little bit like that now, except the man I asked to tip me the wink wasn't an Eastern yogi at the mouth of a holy river but a pugnacious producer of dubious pop records from Coventry. 'It's not a very popular view but the real reason *Pop Idol* worked,' Pete Waterman ended up confiding to me, 'is because we're over-exposed to music.' Now *that* was spot on.

Since the 1950s pop music has become part of everyday existence. I listen to music in the kitchen in the morning giving Sam and Esme breakfast, on my Walkman on the way to work, on the radio in the car at weekends, on the telly as the backing music to adverts and gardening programmes in the evenings. Thankfully, there are different styles of music made to fit all those activities and elements. I often think that music shouldn't be reviewed by genre – sometimes it's hard to keep up with all the proliferating styles of rave or world music anyway – but by the sort of things you use it for. There should be categories of music to dance to, to shag to, to drive to, to sleep to, to cook to. (Hold on. That's Jamie Oliver's idea.) But then, of course, there are subdivisions within those categories. Driving through the city. Driving in the country. Driving to a party. Driving to get back before the babysitter gets the hump. All this is good. Life in the fifties would have been musical purgatory by comparison. It wasn't as if there was something else to listen to if you didn't like Johnnie Ray; well, there was, but it was 'How Much Is That Doggie In The Window'. If you wanted to see what Gene Vincent looked like, you'd have to make sure you caught *Oh Boy*! each week. There wasn't Smash Hits TV.

What I don't do very much is sit down and listen to music. That's the province of classical music enthusiasts (that seems a good word) or teenagers. That's the irony of the situation: there's so much information out there that it's impossible to evaluate what's best to listen to.

Everything gets lost in a wash of information – or turned into white noise. (Which is how My Bloody Valentine sound, come to think of it.) And as an adult now I don't have time to immerse myself in the collected works of The Pixies or whoever their peers today might be.

That means I miss out on the rituals that go along with liking a band too – but really, it isn't an option for me to sign up with S Club Juniors or turn myself into a 'nu metal nutter'. So I've also lost the sense of tribal identity that music once provided. Of course, we now live in a world where a tribal identity can be bought at Top Shop from reading the pages of *Heat* – 'Steal Her Style!' – and that whole culture has been devalued too.

When Elvis stumbled on to a rockin' version of Arthur Crudup's blues number 'That's All Right' in Sam Phillips' Sun Studios in Memphis on 5 July, 1954, he kick-started a revolution felt throughout the southern states, as teenage girls mobbed county fairs to see this white nigger sing, and then across the globe. Succeeding generations have had their hopes and aspirations measured by rock and roll – or reggae or hip hop or whatever other equivalent you choose. The familiar history of rock followed Elvis, as chronicled in the pages of *Mojo*.

But now pop culture seems entirely vapid and more or less indistinguishable from celebrity culture, where stars are evaluated not by a two-page review in *Rolling Stone* or the *NME* but by how many column inches they command in the popular press and how many pages they fill in *Heat*. In fact most pop stars are simply celebrities for whom pop is just another part of a portfolio of assets: they sing, sure, but they can act and dance too, and please give me a role in your film and buy my new line of pants. Lower down on the scale are those pop tarts indistinguishable from the stars of TV shows – even reality TV shows. In fact, with programmes like *Big Brother* and *Popstars*, which have found ways of letting the audience buy into the product, TV is the new pop. It's all too depressing, and symptomatic of a culture growing stoopider.

On a website called CelebMatch.com, you can 'use the scientific method of biorhythms to calculate your most compatible celebrity love'. So I typed in my date of birth and discovered that I had a 96 per cent compatibility match with the supermodel Helena Christensen. Better than that, I scored 99 per cent with Kimberley Davies!

I had no idea who Kimberley Davies might be. One click later I learnt that she and I were 99 per cent intellectually compatible and a 99 per cent physical match too. Emotionally, however, the score was 97 per cent – so I could talk rocket science with her and rewrite the *Kama Sutra*, but we might fall out over who left the freezer door open overnight. Nonetheless, I was eager to find out a bit more about Kim, so clicked on another link and was directed to ten Kimberley Davies-related websites. And only at that point did I log off in disgust with myself.

Are we dumbing down? At the 2001 general election, only 43 per cent of those aged under thirty-five could be bothered to vote. And the BBC Current Affairs Department has had to revise its estimate of the age group that they can't persuade to watch the news any more from eighteen- to twenty-five-year-olds upwards to eighteen- to thirty-five-year-olds.

That's me!

In 2001, for the first time since the war, there were unfilled places at British medical schools, while two universities, Liverpool and Luton, began Media Performance courses. In fact, the number of university places available for those who dream of a career in the media now exceeds those for law, medicine and architecture combined. And over half of all British women in their twenties read a celebrity magazine every week. There's some evidence.

Everything seems easier now – go to Tate Modern and there are helpful wall labels explaining what the paintings and installations are trying to tell us. If you do want to listen to a bit of Wagner, then Classic FM will serve him up in easily digestible portions. And it doesn't matter if you're not familiar with Aeschylus because he's a dead old white man and the great canon of Western literature can be regarded as of marginal relevance to contemporary society, at best. It used to be that everyone knew that *The Ring* was more important than a pop record, and that it made you a better person to know and like the former, not 'How Much Is That Doggie . . .' Now that notion seems absurd.

(If only this were France! They have reality TV, but it's very upmarket. In *La Cinq*, there are five authors under surveillance while they try to write a collective novel while closeted in a country house near Paris. 'We are not influenced by the shallow, sensationalist agenda of *Big Brother*,' said the producer. But then the French always treat even the silly stuff seriously.)

A symptom of this growing idiocy was that upmarket newspapers started to treat programmes like *Big Brother* and *Popstars* and *Pop Idol* seriously as cultural items that need some respect and understanding (to borrow a phrase from Waterman). Good God! Of course half the time they also slammed them. This was a conversation played out on Popbitch:

DUMBING UP
Not to get all Belinda or anything, but can anyone pinpoint the moment when (putatively) smart people became obsessed with thicko culture in a relatively non-ironic way. Spice Girls' first single? It has now got to the point where thicko culture (*Pop Idols*, *Footballers' Wives* etc etc) sets the agenda for the whole country, broadsheets included. Very odd. (fluffer-of-st-george, Mon 25 Feb, 12:40, Reply)

Circa 1964
when there was that Beatles are better than Schubert article in Times (doggo, Mon 25 Feb, 12:40, Reply)

17th Century Dutch 'genre' painters of peasants or bumpkins

with their moralising undertones (idiotmittens, Mon 25 Feb, 12:40, Reply)

Listen 'pal'
If you want to discuss the high art/low art dichotomy in Western culture in the post-Leavisite age of mechanical reproduction then feel free. But for you to use terms like 'thicko culture' it seems that you doth protest too much. (dr-crawdaddy, Mon 25 Feb, 12:40, Reply)

wasn't it when
Family Fortunes stopped displaying the closing credits on Mr Babbage? (bet-lynch-legs, Mon 25 Feb, 12:56, Reply)

People like fun
That's why things have dumbed down. Quite simple really. Also, people have realised that if they sit around discussing Foucault, only 2 people listen to them, and they're both ugly. Whereas if they talk about David Beckham everyone (except for that weird girl) listens. (themanwhofellasleep, Mon 25 Feb, 13:09, Reply)

And a couple of weeks later on the message board:

The high-low mass-debate
When the 'high-low' culture debate started in the '60s, it was actually about high-middle. Dylan?? The Beatles? The difference now is that the middle has gone and people of reasonable intelligence are frantically bottom-feeding, wasting their time on stuff like *Pop Idol*. Thickly ironic or ironically thick? You decide.

(fluffer-of-st-george, Wed 6 Mar, 15:21, Reply)

For better or worse ...
Pop Idol affects how many of the people on this board make their living, so it makes sense that they'd take an interest in it. I found it all too depressing, personally. Nothing exciting or life-affirming about any of it, and surely those things are what make people want to listen to pop in the first place.
(bumpyknuckles, Wed 6 Mar, 15:21, Reply)

The 'highbrow' interest in *Pop Idol* has been a fascination with a new technology the public directly electing future stars for short-lived careers – rather than in the end product. To not be fascinated by *Pop Idol* would be like finding conversations about the invention of television 'stupid' in 1937. It's called keeping up. (lord-venger, Wed 6 Mar, 15:21, Reply)

Pre-cisely
I don't like the insinuation that any interest in 'low-brow' culture is ironic. *Pop Idol* was very compelling TV irrespective of the artistic longevity of the performers. I don't like the idea of snooty high-culture ... Don't play with that garish Fisher-Price train set, play with this elaborately-carved wooden toy that your grandfather gave you.
Ps I make no sense
(themanwhofellasleep, Wed 6 Mar, 15:18, Reply)

Of course, as idiotmittens suggest, there has been a high/low art debate for centuries, and the state and society have always gotten their knickers in a twist over pop culture: newspapers damning jazz as 'jungle music' in the thirties; MPs calling for legislation against Teddy boys, and punks, and ravers; promoters banning acts with their roots in jungle – and garage. That's part of a similarly established distrust of the culturally destabilising effects of democracy. In fact, it was Matthew Arnold in the late nineteenth century and Cambridge don F.R. Leavis in the thirties who established the view that mass civilisation and mass culture threaten, as Leavis said, 'to land us in irreparable chaos'.

Two decades later, even the more sympathetic cultural theorist Richard Hoggart, from the *Lady Chatterley's Lover* trial box, thought most mass entertainments were 'in the end what D.H. Lawrence described as 'anti-life'. They are full of a corrupt brightness, of improper appeals and moral evasions ... they offer nothing which can really grip the brain or heart. They assist a gradual drying-up of the more positive, the fuller, the more cooperative kinds of enjoyment, in which one gains much by giving much.'

It is worth bringing in Hoggart here because he was around at the birth of the British teenager and, for all his stuffy credentials, one of the few people to pay attention to what was going around him at that time (unlike, perhaps, someone like Eliot). The only shame is that he didn't enjoy himself more. Here he is, writing in *The Uses of Literacy* in 1957, about the birth of pop culture as we know it in this country: 'The milk-bars indicate at once, in the nastiness of their modernistic knick-knacks, their glaring showiness, an aesthetic breakdown ... Most of the customers are boys aged between 15 and 20, with drape-suits, picture ties, and an American slouch. Most of them cannot afford a succession of milk-shakes, and make cups of tea serve for an hour or two whilst – and this is their main reason for coming – they put copper after copper into the mechanical record-player ... Compared even with the pub around the corner, this is all a peculiarly thin and pallid form of dissipation, a sort of spiritual dry-rot amid the odour of boiled milk. Many of the customers – their clothes, their hair-styles, their facial expressions all indicate – are living to a large extent in a myth-world compounded of a few simple elements which they take to be those of American life.'

I find it impossible to share Hoggart's pessimism given that we know that pop culture did disrupt the balance sheet. Through the agency of its brightest icons – its idols – it has brought about a world which is more tolerant in every aspect. It's a world where you can walk down the street as a punk – and only get stopped by Japanese tourists to have your picture taken – or smoke a spliff and confess to your fellow MPs without sanction. Where you can play rock and roll without bringing down the forces of government oppression. (In the Middle Ages, the Vatican banned certain arrangements of musical notes, fearing corruption in musical anarchy. And I gather there's been some hoo-hah in Afghanistan recently.) Where you can read about people like you and me in your favourite celebrity magazine rather than some inbred mid-European bunch of royals. Where the nation's pop idol is gay and no one minds.

Ah – but there's the flipside. We never got to see Elvis in the flesh in this country (apart from a stop at Prestwick Airport en route back to Memphis from the army in Germany) but we did see imitators such as Gene Vincent. Even Billy Haley and the Comets visited the mother country – although their promotional trip was a disaster when the expectant Teddy boys saw that Bill was paunchy and middle aged. At least we had Cliff Richard.

But Cliff was never Elvis. He was a poor facsimile, not a rock and roller, a product of the fledgling pop industry. And pop is a rapacious beast. Since the inception of pop culture here in the fifties, pop has latched on to the latest trend, and progressively sucked it dry. The real pop icons of our age like Kylie and Madonna might know nothing about music, but a) all anyone cares about is their latest look and b) it doesn't matter, because someone will hook them up with the best songwriters and the hottest producers, which is the real reason they stay relevant. In fact, rock has a real problem because pop has taken it over and rendered it inert. Hello, Travis! Hello, Coldplay! Hello, Noel and Liam!

Rock stars break down walls and pull down barriers – if often only, it must be conceded, when in desperate straits to find their hidden stash. Pop walks into the room afterwards, and fleeces everyone of their money.

Did Cliff ever fight for any freedoms? No, but The Beatles and the Stones et al. did surely. What's left to fight for now, however? And that's the other problem: the battles rock came here to wage are long since won. But no one seems to have told our contemporary rock icons, so they enact the rituals anyway, puking and fighting, mindless of a higher calling. It makes for a decadent society.

Yet rock is really in danger of becoming a heritage sound – like rock and roll, which in its truest sense only real fans follow, or the blues, or jazz. But pop doesn't mind. It will keep an ear out for the next sound on the street, and then gobble that too. As Cowell said: 'The only way we can know is by keeping in touch with the public.' The worrying thing is, the better the industry is at drilling every cultural oil well, the less gas there will be around to fuel the machine. At some point, you feel, there won't be any styles left to nick, no new sounds to borrow. It will be like the elephant in that Chris Morris set-up on *BrassEye*, with its trunk caught up its anus. Pop will eat itself! (Now, *there* was a shit group.)

Of course, it's the same process that you see in fashion, where companies hire cool-hunters to identify the latest street trends (who cares about haute couture?) and have them made up in the Far East overnight with their own brand logo.

In fact, for all our choice and for all the array of goods in our high-street stores (or on this intraweb thing), there is a relentless drive towards mediocrity. It is a world which sells our children an ersatz version of cultural experiences – like S Club Juniors or *Popstars*. There was never going to be a Woodstock again – or if there was, it was to be Woodstock II, an event created for nostalgic baby-boomers and sponsored and merchandised up to the hilt. (If only it had proved the culture's Altamont.) And for Swinging London in 1966 read Idiot London in 2002. So this is a world where the bland, the imitation of the imitation of the real event, predominates. In its pursuit of the lowest common denominator, pop is a profoundly democratic force, but democracies are boring – decadent but boring. Of course, pop can be political – more political than rock, because it operates almost exclusively through the mass media, so it has a greater window on to our souls – but that always comes at its own price. How do you read Michael Jackson? The oeuvre of the King (was that what he was called last? Supreme Being?) of Pop doesn't look particularly political, although there's clearly a message in a song like 'Black And White', however crassly put. But the very fact of his presence in the charts of every music market on the planet for the best part of three decades has surely done more to dismantle notions of racism than the work of someone like Billy Bragg. (Apologies, Billy, always liked your records.) By this reading, Wacko is the most radical pop act or performance artist in history, because he has even turned his own body into a piece of work in which racial and sexual distinctions are no longer apparent. Yet Wacko is able to sell so many records around the world precisely because he is such a polymorphous figure, equally acceptable everywhere. (Even if every Pulp fan thinks he's a freek, they're still in the minority.)

(There's a nice footnote to Wacko Jacko's story. In 1981 he placed a phone call to a new British pop star. The voice on the other end of the line thought it was a prank and told him to fuck off. The producer of Jackson's latest work-in-progress tried again: 'This is Quincy Jones and that really is Michael Jackson.' This time Adam Ant took the call. Michael wanted to know where Adam got his Hussar stage jacket and drum sound from. Jackson's new album? *Thriller*, which turned out to be the biggest selling album in pop history, in no small measure thanks to the incendiary videos, in which Michael dressed in his own military uniform. Fortunately, Quincy didn't bother with the Ants' percussion side of things.)

Britain has actually always been more of a pop country than America. Pop acts have traditionally never placed much emphasis on the business of live performance. Their pact with the public is made through the mass media – radio and TV (and film) and the teen and tabloid press. A new pop sensation can easily seize the public imagination: all you need is for the record company to shell out enough moolah to advertise the product, so that it hits the Top 10, and then sleep with a donkey (or suchlike) to make it to the front of the tabloids. Without truly national newspapers or a big TV pop show, the route to celebrity is harder for a music act in America, which is why

Oasis always struggled there and why America always preferred rock to pop, until the advent of MTV. And *American Idol*.

This is also why the biggest pop stars in this country have usually loved telly. Cliff became famous in the fifties through his exposure on the television; Kylie and Jason owed the huge size of their initial fan base in the eighties to *Neighbours*; and S Club 7 became a teen phenomenon in the nineties through their own children's telly show. And hi there, Gareth.

If you want to understand Cliff's contemporary popularity, in fact, look at the BPI handbook for 2001. There's a chart with the Top 10 music-related TV programmes, and second in the table (behind the Brit Awards) is *The Cliff Richard Story*, an ITV production which drew 8.46 million viewers. Then at seven is *A Song for Jill*. This BBC show was a musical tribute to the murdered Jill Dando and featured Cliff heavily, as one of her favourite artists. Then, two places lower down, there's *An Audience with Cliff Richard*, which pulled in 5.25 million viewers. That's good going. And it probably wasn't just pensioners watching. It's worth pointing out that *The Cliff Richard Story* was broadcast in the middle of the week and after 10 p.m. (*Popstars* and the S Club 7 series didn't qualify for the chart, but got their own separate mentions in the accompanying text.)

The alarming point about television, however, is not that Cliff is such an ubiquitous presence, but something far more worrying. With its screaming fans and hand-wringing/knicker-wetting media coverage, *Big Brother* could be The Beatles all over again. There's even an element of public participation – we can have our say. In a way, all popular culture is about getting the audience involved. That's why we have the charts. That's why we prefer big cinemas. Now, with *Big Brother*, the screen of the box in the corner of the room has been breached.

So pop music's fundamental problem isn't that there's too much of it, it's that over the last fifty years there's been an explosion in the growth of pop culture as a whole, and now pop is losing its primacy in that culture. When the contestants from *Big Brother* leave the house they don't return to real life, they go razzing it at shampoo product launches in the company of other TV starlets and wimpering pop idols and celebrity chefs and gardeners. If they're lucky, the tabs will have their people there. It's the culture of gossip and celebrity which calls the shots now. We are living in a myth-world compounded of a few simple elements which we take to be those of fame and fortune.

I loved *Big Brother*, and can't see that watching it is bad for my health. (My friend Jeremy has a very good Law of Television which states that there's good TV and bad TV. Bad TV is the sort of stuff that actually makes you stupider when you're watching it – like 'those Stop, Police! sort of programmes presented by someone like Shaw Taylor'; good TV is stuff that . . . doesn't.) If it was, all the same, I could simply switch channels.

Yet the terrifying thing about pop culture as a whole is that it doesn't stop moving. The real danger of *Big Brother* and other reality shows was that their very success seemed to endanger other television programmes. The Independent Televison Commission's annual report for 2001 complained that shows on current affairs, the arts, religion and regional affairs were 'threatened species' because they were unattractive to commercial broadcasters obsessed by high ratings. 'Competition for peak-time audiences, in particular, can impact on diversity, as can the attention given to the pursuit of viewers in the 16–34 age range,' it intoned. Hey! That was me they were talking about again! 'This is evidenced,' it continued, 'by the preponderance of similar programme formats across channels, the tendency to exhaust generic series, whether Top 10s and other "list" programmes or ". . . from Hells", and a reliance – whether through overt or covert filming – on programmes observing and revealing coarse behaviour.' 'Coarse': lovely.

The report argued that there were real losers in this war with Reithian values. 'The battleground that is peak-time inevitably diverts resources and attention away from other day parts and viewers looking for engaging and fresh material in day time are suffering particularly badly.'

Pop eats everything – and this was pop TV in action.

It's so many channels, nothing worth watching. So many records, nothing worth listening to. Yadda yadda.

It was the great French Situationist Guy Debord – inspiration to The Sex Pistols and also, it seems, The Stone Roses – who said things like 'Culture turned completely into commodity must also turn into the star commodity of the spectacular society . . . In the second half of this century culture will hold the key role in the development of the economy . . .' There's a dollop of that thinking in the mind of the Chancellor, Gordon Brown, and in the work of Debord's fellow countryman, Jean Baudrillard, who is the pop idol of modern cultural theory (following on from old fogeys like Arnold). He talks about the 'hyperreal' world in which we now live, where it is impossible to distinguish between reality and the artificial. In the past, the media were believed to mirror, reflect or represent reality. That's what *Big Brother* says it does on the tin. But now the media are coming to constitute a hyperreality that's more real than real. That's what *Big Brother* is.

According to Baudrillard, the surfeit of information with which we are bombarded across the media these days turns information into its own white noise. 'Information is directly destructive of meaning and signification, or neutralizes it,' he has written. 'The loss of meaning is directly linked to the dissolving and dissuasive action of information, the media and the mass media . . . Information dissolves meaning and the social into a sort of nebulous state leading not at all to a surfeit of innovation but to the very contrary, to total entropy.' Blimey. But who can say that following *Big Brother* doesn't exactly involve that experience?

In fairness to Germaine Greer, she stumbled on to much the same point in her *Big Brother* essay for the *Observer*. Concluding her piece pessimistically, citing the work of Mona Hatoum, she argued that if we actively seek television images of the insides of our bodies it must be because this is the only kind of evidence that we trust to prove that we are real. 'Reality television is not the end of civilisation as we know it; it is civilisation.' And so: 'Television has become more real than real life.' Well, that seems about right.

To turn the pretension level up one to eleven, it's worth hearing about one other foreign thinker, and calling another character to the stand. Will Young: 'As Adorno said, everything in music is made up to be inspirational and on the spot, but post '20s it's down to one beat and you don't get anything original.' William! He was talking to *Time Out* as I was finishing writing most of this book. It was Jubilee week, and the nation's pop idol was playing at the Queen's party at Buck Palace, along with Sir Paul McCartney and Sir Elton John, as well as other Simon Fuller acts S Club 7 and Emma 'Baby Spice' Bunton. Will posed for the cover of the magazine painted head to toe in gold, and bearing a globe upon his shoulders. Or the weight of the Earth. The headline? 'Goldenballs' – presumably some kind of reference to the England football captain, whose wife had called him that. Inside he was still semi-naked, with, disconcertingly, jeans so low so you could see a big golden bush of pubic hair protruding at his waistline. Will! I was shocked. Shocked that such a nice boy should portray himself like this. And worried, for him, about what his parents might say.

'We know when we watch films,' he continued, 'there's this basic formula – the baddie, the goodie and the girl. So you congratulate yourself because you've worked out the ending before you get to it. It's the same thing in music. I'm not criticising it, because it fulfils. In fact, people could say the same thing about my music . . . But it serves a purpose.'

Perhaps it's come to a funny pass when my pop idol is better read than me. But perhaps this is just the sort of stuff that I wanted to hear from Will, because I thought it would make Simon Cowell quail.

As far as I know, Theodor Adorno was a German philosopher, something to do with the Frankfurt School before the war, who also complained about the advent of mass culture. His answer to the problem was to grapple with the avant-garde. To understand a work of art you need to engage with it, and so if everything looks as if it's been done before, you need to find something with a challenge, something worthy of your time and mental faculties.

That's a good solution, and I've wondered whether the next culture to be stormed by pop culture will be the classical music market. I don't mean Russell Watson (the opera singer and entertainment at the Beckhams' World Cup leaving party) or The Opera Babes invading the charts. I mean that classical music is one of the few cultural wellsprings left, because it makes such demands on its listeners. If I were a teenager wanting to define myself against the conformity of Coldplay or Slipknot, just as much as Will or Gareth, I'd be tempted to stake out some of that territory for myself. (I grew up in the era of Aled Jones, however, so again for me it's not an option.)

Will's still at it. 'Through mass popular culture,' he told his clearly startled interviewer, 'you can make positive changes. I know this makes me sound like a campaigner for goodness. But why am I here? I don't know where I got my voice from . . . but you have to look beyond it and see what your responsibilities are.'

Is he right? Can mass popular culture make a change for good? Or is that opportunity circumscribed by its very nature? Does it matter? Sometimes I think it's better to go with the flow, as Richard Hoggart might have. Relax. (Look! Listen! VIBRATE!) Smile. Again towards the end of writing this book, I read on the website Ananova that Gareth Gates was going to launch 'Gareth Cam' on Smash Hits TV, which meant daily broadcasts from Gareth's personal life – as filmed by Gareth himself. Fantastic.

But isn't writing a great song as hard as scoring a vocal work like one of Schoenberg's? Or, at least, doesn't it deserve the same respect? Because if pop songs find a place in your heart, whatever the medium in which they reach you, doesn't that cut through all that Baudrillard cock-and-bull? The real reason I wish the best for Will is nothing to do with the fact that he can string a sentence together; it's to do with the fact that he can sing a song.

I agree that contemporary life often feels like a dream sequence in which it's hard to know what to feel. I'm not sure whether I care about the contestants on *Big Brother*, or in fact can tell whether they're even really real. For a long time I wasn't sure why I liked indie music, the music of my youth. For a long time, I wasn't sure why I loved my first *Pop Idol*.

But then I asked Pete Waterman.

So why did I love *Pop Idol*? It was a TV programme that looked as trashy as the next. It looked as if it would produce just another hopeless pop star, who would spend his days filling the pages of *Heat*. But it worked because of the music on the show. So it stuck two fingers up to telly and TV culture. And in doing so, it reminded me of the power of song.

'There's far too much of music that's treated lightly,' Waterman said. 'There's music everywhere, so it becomes a little bit wallpaper. I'm talking generally. Music is now a part of cultural life. And what we've done in the last ten years is water it down even more, so music isn't as special as it was in the fifties – and the last time it was really special was probably the sixties. It isn't any longer the preserve of people who like music; it's been stretched out.'

The key to getting *Pop Idol* right was in some ways rather boring and technical. There was too much music on telly, but none of it was any good. *Top of the Pops* had lost its popular appeal – moved to Friday nights, changed its musical philosophy, not like the old days when 'the kids watched the bands, and Dad looks at the legs on Pan's People'. But *Pop Idol* made music feel special again, limiting access to the singers to one hour a week, at least in the latter half of the show, with the live Saturday night broadcasts. It was to this end that Henry's House restricted press access to the final ten. All of this went against current thinking about our pop culture.

But the secret to the whole thing was making sure the music worked. Cue Waterman's participation. And the reason that the music worked is that music does work. It's an incredibly powerful force.

> *'That is the hardest job in the frigging world'* – Waterman

'If I could sit down tomorrow and write a song which went "Each morning I wake up/And start to put on my make-up/I say a little prayer for you . . ." I would make another million pounds,' Pete Waterman said to me. 'I don't need to make a million-pound video; I don't need to be good looking; I don't need to be white; I don't need to be Asian; all I need to do is wake up and go "Each morning I wake up/And start to put on my make-up" . . . That's all I have to do.

'And that is the hardest job in the frigging world. To wake up in the morning and write a song that everyone goes 'Oh . . .'. It's easy to wake up and hire the video director of the moment and give him a million pounds to make a video. He'll take your money. It's easy to wake up tomorrow and get a clever graphic artist to do you a clever graphic. You'll give him a hundred grand, that's easy. It's easy to set up a website. That's easy.'

It's lovely to think of him there, grappling with his own art . . .

'"Each morning I wake up/And start to put on my make-up" . . . I've sat here for thirty frigging years waiting to wake up and put on my make-up. I fucking still ain't done it. I come back to the table every day of my life, waiting for that line to come, and you know what, the minute that line comes, I'll retire, 'cos it will never happen again.

'And I've still never done it.'

But I sincerely hope he does.

Epilogue:

AND IN THE END

> *'The great rock and roll, you might not hear it again. Like the horse and buggy'* – Bob Dylan

I'd like this to be like those secret tracks you sometimes find at the end of a CD. These thoughts, I fear, might be the intoxicated folk-scratchings at the end of The Stone Roses' *Second Coming* . . .

In the same period of my life as I was reading *Heat* and watching *Big Brother* and *Pop Idol*, I also became immersed in Bob Dylan's work. I had always liked him as a kid, because my parents played him around the house, and I liked him as a teenager, when I dug his attitude, and found satisfaction in placing his oeuvre in my mental chart of pop's history. But I didn't really get to love him until recently, which was when I started really listening, up late at night, on my own. (Now I have an entirely separate section on my CD shelves for Bob alone.)

The genius of Bob Dylan isn't in the life, it's in the songs. He knows that. I think, in fact, his best album isn't one with his own songs, but *World Gone Wrong*, one of two acoustic albums of country, blues and folk standards that he recorded in the mid-nineties, and released to howls of derision. The songs, when you listen, are extraordinary. The way he sings them is beyond words.

In the mid-eighties, when corporate rock was on the rise, Dylan observed, in his usual clear fashion, 'There's an old saying, "If you want to defeat your enemy, sing his song" and that's pretty much still true. I think it's happened and nobody knows the difference ... The great folk music and the great rock and roll, you might not hear it again. Like the horse and buggy.' In other words, Springsteen and friends were being lured off the righteous path by the pop industry. And the great rock and roll would be forgotten if people forgot what was really great about it first time round.

There's a final contradiction in the pop song that I think is worth mentioning, all the same.

Pop songs are made to be transitory. But they stay fixed with us. Whether bad, or good. And they provide us with a memory of the time when we first heard that song. Perhaps a TV programme can do that just as effectively. As Simon Fuller said, The Monkees were crap, really, but you look at the show, and it takes you back to the sixties.

Perhaps *Pop Idol* was crap, really. But I think *Pop Idol* captured its moment in time, the time when Britain began a madcap fling with a new kind of entertainment and a new cultural feeling in the air. It will also remind me of a time in my own life, when I was thirty-one, with two small children, with Zoë, and happy. A time when I was old enough to feel nostalgia for the pop hits of my youth, and a time when I knew there were more important things in life than pop music.

AUTHOR'S NOTE: Records To Listen to While Writing a Book

Adam and the Ants, *Antbox*, Columbia, 2000
Berlioz, *Les Nuits d'Eté*, HMV Classics, 2001
Big Star, *#1 Record/Radio City*, Big Beat, 1992
The Blind Boys of Alabama, *Spirit of the Century*, Real World Records, 2001
Blue, *All Rise*, Virgin, 2001
David Bowie, *Diamond Dogs*, EMI, 1999; *Scary Monsters*, EMI, 1999; *Heathen*, Columbia, 2002
Butthole Surfers, *Electriclarryland*, Capitol, 1996
The Charlatans, *Tellin' Stories*, Beggars Banquet, 1997; *Us And Us Only*, Universal/MCA, 1999; *Wonderland*, Universal/MCA, 2001
Bobby Darin, *Dream Lover*, Delta, 1998
DJ Shadow, *The Private Press*, Universal/MCA, 2002
Destiny's Child, *Survivor*, Columbia, 2001
Brian Eno, David Byrne, *My Life In The Bush of Ghosts*, E.G./Virgin, 1998
Hear'Say, *Popstars*, Polydor 2001
I Am Kloot, *Natural History*, Wall of Sound, 2001
Eleni Karaindrou, *Trojan Women*, ECM New Series, 2002

Lambchop, *Is A Woman*, City Slang, 2002
Little Axe, *Slow Fuse*, Wired, 1996
Minotaur Shock, *Chiff-Chaffs and Willow Warblers*, Melodic, 2001
New Order, *Technique*, London, 1989
Arvo Pärt, *Sanctuary*, Virgin Classics,
The Pixies, *Death to the Pixies*, 4AD, 1997
Public Enemy, *Fear Of A Black Planet*, Def Jam, 1995
Cliff Richard, *The Rock 'n' Roll Years*, EMI, 1998
Johnnie Ray, *The Best of Johnnie Ray*, Columbia, 1996
S Club 7, *Sunshine*, Polydor, 2001
Sloan, *Between The Bridges*, Murder/Universal, 1999
The Smiths, *Singles*, WEA, 1995
Bruce Springsteen, *18 Tracks*, Columbia, 2001
The Stone Roses, *The Second Coming*, Geffen, 1997; *The Remixes*, Silvertone, 2000
Dickie Valentine, *The Best of Dickie Valentine*, Castle Pulse, 1998
Various Artists, *Gone Where They Don't Play Billiards: Music and Mirth from the Halls on Phonograph Cylinders*, Cylidisc
V/A, *Avalon Blues: The Music of Mississippi John Hurt*, Vanguard, 2001
V/A, *The Rough Guide To Bluegrass*, World Music Network, 2001
V/A, *The Travelling Record Man*, Ace, 2001
V/A, *Beyond Nashville*, Manteca, 2001
V/A, *The Best Punk Anthems in the World . . . Ever!*, Virgin, 1998

V/A, *Soul Time Volume 3*, Epic
V/A, *Modrophenia*, Global TV, 1997
V/A, *The Score*, Mojo
V/A, *Cafe del Mar: Volumen Dos*, React, 1995
V/A, *Cafe del Mar: Volumen Tres*, React, 1996
V/A, *The Yemen Tihama*, Topic, 2002
V/A, *Pop Idol: The Big Band Album*, BMG/RCA/S Records, 2002
Gillian Welch, *Hell Among the Yearlings*, Acony Sounds, 1998
David Whitfield, *David Whitfield's Greatest Hits*, Decca, 1990
Wilco, *Being There*, Warner Bros., 1997; *Yankee Hotel Foxtrot*, Nonesuch, 2002

Caspar Llewellyn Smith

BIBLIOGRAPHY

Heiner Bastian, *Warhol*, Tate Gallery Publishing, 2002
Jean Baudrillard, *Screened Out*, Verso Books, 2002
Kim Cooper and David Smay, *Bubblegum Music Is the Naked Truth*, Feral House, 2001
Mark Ellingham and John Buckley, *The Rough Guide to Rock*, Rough Guides, 1999
Jeff Evans, *The Guinness Television Encyclopedia*, Guinness, 1995
Peter Everett, *You'll Never Be 16 Again*, BBC, 1986
Charlie Gillett (ed.) and Simon Frith (ed.), *The Beat Goes On*, Pluto Press, 1996
Fred Goodman, *The Mansion on the Hill*, Jonathan Cape, 1997
Jonathon Green, *All Dressed Up*, Jonathan Cape, 1999
Hugh Gregory, *A Century of Pop*, Hamlyn, 1998
Robert Hewison, *Culture and Consensus*, Methuen Publishing Ltd, 1997
Peter Hillmore, *Live Aid: The Concert*, Sidgwick and Jackson, 1985
Richard Hoggart, *The Way We Live Now*, Chatto and Windus, 1995
Andrew Hussey, *The Game of War*, Jonathan Cape,

2001

Myleene Klass et al, *Hear'Say: Our Story*, Granada, 2001

Naomi Klein, *No Logo*, Flamingo, 2001

Hanif Kureishi (ed.) and Jon Savage (ed.), *The Faber Book of Pop*, Faber and Faber, 1995

Colin Larkin (ed.), *The Virgin Encyclopedia of Popular Music*, Virgin, 2002

Jon E. Lewis and Penny Stempel, *Cult TV*, Pavilion Books, 1993

Colin MacInnes, *The Colin MacInnes Omnibus*, Allison and Busby, 1985

Maria Malone, *Popstars: The Making of Hear'Say*, Granada, 2001

Hugh Massingberd (ed.), *The Daily Telegraph Book of Obituaries*, Macmillan, 1995

Ivo Mosley (ed.), *Dumbing Down*, Imprint Academic, 2000

Brian Moynahan, *The British Century*, Weidenfeld and Nicolson, 1997

Simon Napier-Bell, *Black Vinyl, White Powder*, Ebury Press, 2001

Philip Norman, *Shout! The True Story of The Beatles*, Corgi, 1982

Alex Ogg with David Upshall, *The Hip Hop Years: A History of Rap*, Channel 4 Books, 1999

Sian Pattenden, *How To Make It in the Music Business*, Virgin Books, 1998

Dick Pountain and David Robins, *Cool Rules*, Foci, 2000

Tim Rice, *The Guinness Book of Number One Hits*, Guinness, 1994

Jean Ritchie, *Big Brother: The Unseen Story*, Channel 4 Books, 2000

David Roberts, *Guinness World Records: British Hit Singles*, Gullane Publishing, 2002

Chris Rojek, *Celebrity*, Foci, 2001

Dafydd Rees and Luke Crampton, *The Guinness Book of Rock Stars*, Gullane Publishing, 1994

Jon Savage, *Time Travel*, Chatto and Windus, 1996

John Seabrook, *Nobrow*, Methuen Publishing Ltd, 2000

Sian Solanas, *Pop Idol: The Inside Story of TV's Biggest Ever Search for a Superstar*, Carlton Books, 2002

John Storey, *Cultural Theory and Popular Culture*, Prentice Hall, 2000

Pete Waterman, *I Wish I Was Me*, Virgin Books, 2000

Will Young, *Anything Is Possible*, Contender Books, 2002